ROMAN EMPIRE

Camelot
EDITORA

SCAN HERE TO GET TO
KNOW OUR BOOKS!

President: Paulo Roberto Houch
MTB 0083982/SP

Editorial Coordination: Paola Houch
Translation: Priscilla Pellegrino
Art Coordination: Rubens Martim
Editorial Production: Ana Vasconcelos (ECO Editorial)
Layout: Patrícia Andrioli
Images: Shutterstock (page 67 - Shutterstock/Viacheslav Lopatin)

Legal deposit has been made.

All rights reserved to
IBC – Instituto Brasileiro de Cultura LTDA
CNPJ 04.207.648/0001-94
Avenida Juruá, 762 – Alphaville Industrial
CEP. 06455-010 – Barueri/SP
Sales: Tel.: +55 (11) 3393-7727 (comercial2@editoraonline.com.br)
www.editoraonline.com.br

Contents

ALL ROADS LEAD TO ROME!

We can begin the list of legacies from languages: Portuguese, for example, is derived from Latin, the language which was written and spoken in Rome. We continue with the Roman numerals, represented by seven of the alphabet letters, which we also know. Law influenced and gave rise to legal codes, adopted in Western societies. In the arts, the Romans were influenced by the Greeks, and were masters in reproducing the human figure. In Florence, the Renaissance was one of the richest periods in the whole history of art, with masters like Leonardo Da Vinci, Michelangelo and Botticelli enchanting humanity.

The paths of the Roman Empire, in politics, economics, arts, culture, architecture, religion and much more, can be found here in this book. And speaking of "paths", the expression "all roads lead to Rome" dates back to the 1st century, when the Roman Empire extended from Britain to Persia (present-day England to Iran), and reached an incredible 49 thousand miles of roads, composing important means of communication, through which messengers issued orders throughout the empire.

Dive into the wealth, history, achievements and secrets of the Roman Empire.

1

FROM VILLAGE TO POWER

THE EMERGENCE OF ROME, IN CENTRAL ITALY, DATES FROM THE 8TH CENTURY BCE, A PERIOD WHEN THE FUTURE EMPIRE WAS JUST A SMALL GROUP OF DIVERSE PEOPLES

In general, modern historians consider the emergence of the city of Rome during the 8th century BCE as a small village in the center of Italy. Those lands in the Italian peninsula had been inhabited since the first millennium before Christ by various peoples. These populations made use of the fertile soil and the very mild climate of the region. Among them were Umbrian, Sabine and Latin tribes, which established agricultural and pastoral villages.

Experts emphasize that Rome began through the merger of a group of seven Latin and Sabine villages, all of them located on the banks of the Tiber River. These peoples had a very close relationship with the Greeks - founders of colonies located to the south of that peninsula - and with the Etruscans, established to the north.

ANCESTORS

According to Harvard University professor and historian Thomas R. Martin, the main evidence of the immediate ancestors of the Romans comes from the archaeological excavation of tombs – dating back to the 9th and 8th centuries BCE – of the people later called Villanovans.

However, there is no reason to believe that these populations, inhabiting different communities, could be classified as a unified or homogeneous group. On the other hand, studies clearly highlight that these people engaged in rudimentary agricultural activities and horse breeding as well.

GREEKS

In the eighth century BCE, the Romans and other peoples of southern and central Italy were already in frequent contact with many merchants from Greece who traveled to the Italian territory by sea. Such economic exchange substantially contributed to the growth of Roman society and culture.

A considerable number of Greeks settled in the region in the same period in search of opportunities to become rich through agriculture. As a result, some cities predominantly populated by Greek citizens became, years later, extremely significant communities. Some examples are Sicily and Naples.

The proximity to Greek culture created an effect on the development of the Roman way of life, which was inspired by models of literature, theater, and also architecture. However, while Greece influenced and was the object of constant admiration by the inhabitants of Rome, it was also undervalued due to its political disunity and military inferiority.

ETRUSCANS

There is much debate regarding the influence of the Etruscans on Roman life. Some groups of scholars believe that these people, located north of Rome, may have been the most relevant external force to affect Roman ways. Some experts have even speculated that they may have con-

Temple in Sicily, Italy, shows Greek influence on Roman formation

*Bust of Herodotus: historian believed that Etruscans
came from Lydia, in Anatolia*

Archaeologists elucidate that the Etruscan people used to bury their dead in underground tombs built in the form of replicas – on a smaller scale – of the houses where they lived when alive. They covered the inside of the residence with paintings portraying mythological and everyday episodes. The families of this population also adorned the burial places with personal and decorative objects. The objective was always the same: to reproduce the comfort of real life in the tombs.

quered ancient Rome, with Etruscan kings ruling the new city in the later part of the monarchy.

Nevertheless, knowledge of the origins of Etrurian men and women remains extremely limited. Partly because historians understand only a small portion of their language, which is probably not Indo-European.

In the 5th century BCE, the historian Herodotus claimed that the Etruscans had emigrated from Lydia in Anatolia to the region that is now Italy. However, Dionysius of Halicarnassus rejected this hypothesis, stating that the Italian territory had always been the true home of this population.

In any case, it is now known that the Etruscans did not form a unified ethnic or political country. They lived in numerous independent cities grouped on the hills of central Italy.

Culturally, they produced artworks considered very refined for their time, such as jewelry and sculptures. However, they spent a considerable amount of money on importing luxurious objects from the Mediterranean region, especially from the Greeks. The Etruscans, in fact, maintained a close relationship with the Greek inhabitants at the time and adapted that culture to their own. An example of this are the famous Greek vases, found intact in Etruscan tombs

Archaeological works show that the Roman ancestors manufactured metal weapons, as well as other bronze and iron objects. As bronze is, basically, a mixture of copper and brass, and as brass was only mined in places very far from Italy, these populations most likely practiced sophisticated long-distance trade.

MONARCHY

The initial Roman governmental configuration was a monarchy. Basically, the king was chosen by the Senate, composed of a kind of council of noble elders and heads of aristocratic families. The monarch exercised judicial, administrative, legislative, military and even religious functions. Nonetheless, for decisions considered more relevant, the king would consult with the senators.

Historians emphasize that during this two-and-a-half-century period of history, seven kings ruled Rome, with Romulus as pioneer. Of these, the first four ones were Sabines and Latins, while the last three were of Etruscan origin.

DEVELOPMENT

In general, this group of monarchs was responsible for urban development and Roman strengthening. Gradually, Rome became a larger settlement and more capable of protecting itself from potential attacks through a strategy focused on two fronts: the absorption of other peoples and the arrangement of alliances with neighboring societies to create military cooperation.

Time proved that this tactic came to be the most correct one, as it was responsible for forming the foundation of long-term Roman expansion. The incorporation of foreigners was practically a survival necessity for a community like Rome, which had such a fragile and small beginning.

Furthermore, this strategy was an innovation in the ancient world. Not even the Greeks or any other groups of the time implemented a similar policy. The truth is that the city-states of Ancient Greece rarely allowed an outsider to become a citizen. The Greek world employed the advent of citizenship only as a way to honor a wealthy foreigner who had benefited the community and did not need or intend to become an ordinary citizen.

Thus, the new and exclusive Roman policy of welcoming foreigners with open arms to increase the number of citizens was the secret to becoming the most powerful State the planet has ever seen.

The action was so essential that the Roman government even offered the chance of upward social mobility to slaves. Roman nobles had slaves as their property, just as in all other ancient societies. At that time, slaves were considered mere property and not human beings. They gained the opportunity to earn citizenship rights after the period of freedom. Someone became a slave by being captured in war, sold on the international market by invaders who had kidnapped them, or by being born to a slave mother. This servant could buy their freedom with earnings the master allowed them to accumulate in order to stimulate harder work or they could also receive freedom as a gift in the owner's will.

It is worth highlighting that a freed slave had legal obligations to their former owner in a patronage relationship. Yet, freed men and women, as they were officially designated, had full civil rights, such as legal marriage. While they could not be elected to political offices or serve in the army, their children became Roman citizens with full rights.

As in many other cases, a legend provided an ancient origin for this rather unusual policy of foreigners' inclusion. According to the story, Romulus realized that Rome, after its founding, could not grow or safeguard itself because it lacked women to give birth to the necessary number of children to increase its population. Thereby, he supposedly sent representatives to neighboring societies to request the right for his men, regardless of their social class, to marry women from any nearby communities. Romulus instructed the messengers to say that, even though the community of Rome was small at that time, the gods had granted it a pretty prosperous future.

Yet, all the neighboring peoples reportedly rejected the request for matrimonial alliances. With no other option, the king decided to prepare a rather risky plan. He would have women kidnapped. To this end, he invited the Sabine people to a religious festival in Rome and abducted all the unmarried girls.

The episode caused a bloody battle between the two neighboring communities. However, amidst the war, the Sabine brides allegedly rushed towards the combatants, causing the fight to pause. In that way, the new wives of the Romans pleaded with both groups to stop fighting and make peace. Otherwise, they could kill them right there. Faced with their plea, Romans and Sabines ceased the battle and merged the two populations into an expanded Roman State

The legend manages to explain, through the role of women in this specific incident, how immigration and the assimilation of other peoples formed the foundation of power in Ancient Rome. The story also highlights the traditional Roman ideal of women as being the mothers of Roman citizens, willing even to courageously sacrifice themselves for the survival of their community.

EXPANSION

The foreigners' inclusion policy had such a significant effect that the Roman population grew considerably over two centuries. In this period, the territory already covered approximately 300 square miles of the Lazio region, enough agricultural land to support up to 40,000 families.

Probably, by means of specialized services of Etruscan engineers, in the 6th century BCE, the Romans drained the open section at the bottom of the Palatine and Capitoline Hills, which had previously been swampy, to become the city center. The newly created space, named Roman Forum, remained the most historic and symbolic section of Rome for a thousand years.

Its construction as a meeting place for political, legal and commercial matters, as well as for public funerals and festivals, occurred almost simultaneously with the Athenians creating the Agora in Greece to serve as an open public center. It demonstrates the common cultural developments happening in the Mediterranean region at that time.

Over the years, new and large buildings were built around the Forum. These structures were used for meetings among authorities, trial proceedings and government administrative functions.

KINGS

The king figure held a strong value in Ancient Rome. Monarchs were recognized as famous founders of lasting traditions. One example is Numa Pompilius, the second to ascend to the throne (ruled from 715 BCE to 673 BCE), who became famous for establishing public religious rituals and priesthoods that venerated the gods to support Rome.

Tullus Hostilius succeeded Numa Pompilius and ruled from 673 BCE to 641 BCE. He gained more notoriety due to his wars with Alba Longa, Fidenae and Veii, which marked the first territorial conquests in Latin lands and the first expansion beyond the walls of Rome.

Ancus Marcius assumed the kingship of Rome after the death of Tullus Hostilius and remained in power for 25 years. Known for achieving peaceful administration, he was the last king of Sabine origin. He structured the city by building aqueducts, founding the port of Ostia and erecting the first wooden bridge over the Tiber River.

After Ancus Marcius' death, Tarquin Priscus went to the Comitia Curiata – the popular assembly – and managed to convince its members that he should be elected king instead of the deceased monarch's sons, as they were still adolescents. Hence, Tarquin succeeded Ancus Marcius. He ascended the throne in 616 BCE and continued to rule until 578 BCE when he was allegedly killed in a conspiracy orchestrated by the three sons of Ancus Marcius.

Servius Tullius, also Etruscan, was Tarquin Priscus' son-in-law and ascended to power through the influence of his mother-in-law, Tanaquil.

The Roman Forum was the space for political, legal and commercial meetings in Ancient Rome

Today, the Roman Forum presents a cluster of ruins from centuries of history. Little or almost nothing remains of the architecture of that time. Even so, a tour of the site places the tourist in an environment filled with Rome's golden moments.

He ruled from 578 BCE to 535 BCE. He became famous for creating basic institutions to organize Roman citizens into groups for political and military purposes, as well as successfully introducing the practice of granting citizenship to freed slaves.

The seventh and last Roman king before the establishment of the republic was Tarquin, the Proud. He ascended to the throne in 535 BCE and left it in 509 BCE when a series of events led to his deposition and the end of the first monarchical period in Rome.

SOCIAL STRUCTURE

Most of the Romans believed that the region took the form of a community in the 8th century BCE when it was under the rule of kings. This was said to be the first monarchical period of Rome. However, modern historians conclude that little is known about the events of the formative period of the local history.

Yet, the legends surrounding the monarchy of that time demonstrate the existence of significant ideas Roman citizens had about their origins.

Such lines of thought help to understand the structure of politics and society even in the later times of the republic; the system emerged in the late 6th century BCE once the monarchy was overthrown. A curious fact is that the Romans, for the rest of their history, referred to the government as republican, even after the restoration of the monarchy in the Empire.

The Roman technical term for the political community as a whole was "Roman people" (populus Romanus), but, in reality, this definition did not suggest a democratic environment. The fact is that the ruling class almost always held the reins of the local government. Just like in the contemporary global society, a few families had political and economic control within the Roman scene.

Therefore, the plebeians, the majority of the population - composed of artisans, merchants, and peasants - lived in uncomfortable social conditions. The clients, free and poor individuals, depended on the patrician families, to whom they regularly provided favors, services and political and military support. In return, they received economic assistance and protection. The more clients a patrician had under their protection, the more political and social importance they gained. Finally, slaves, generally war prisoners or indebted individuals, constituted a less numerous portion of the population in the monarchical period.

Legend has it that King Tullus Hostilius, the third monarch of Rome, died after being struck by lightning as punishment for his pride.

2

REPUBLICAN ROME

THE OPPOSITION OF THE ARISTOCRACY MADE THE MONARCHIC PERIOD FAIL IN ROMAN TERRITORY AND PAVED THE WAY FOR A NEW FORM OF GOVERNMENT

It seemed that everything was favorable for the Roman monarchy. It was practically a consensus that Servius Tullius – ruler between 578 BCE and 535 BCE – had laid solid foundations for organizing Roman citizens into groups for political and military purposes. The idea of granting citizenship to freed slaves also seemed to be an important step toward consolidating the regime.

Nevertheless, monarchs started having their power threatened by the wealthier classes. This direct opposition exerted strong pressure since the wealthy families considered themselves socially equivalent to the king and therefore sought more status and power in their hands. The support that common people gave to the monarch also deeply bothered them.

This cold war placed the kings in a position of absolute insecurity because there was a fear that a more powerful member of the upper class might resort to violence to seize the throne. In search of support against such individuals, the monarchs often had as important allies citizens who had enough money to supply them with weapons but were not wealthy enough to be part of the upper class.

Despite this safeguard, some of the wealthiest Romans managed to depose King Tarquin the Proud in 509 BCE. He lost the throne due to an incident involving Lucretia. This peculiar woman of Rome's upper class had allegedly been raped by the king's son after being threatened with a knife. Although her husband and father had asked her not to blame her-

Painting by Spaniard Eduardo Rosales depicts the suicide of Lucretia, which culminated in the fall of the monarchy and the institution of the republican period in Rome

self for the incident, Lucretia committed suicide. However, before her death, she asked her relatives to avenge her.

The deposition of Tarquin was led by Lucius Junius Brutus, who succeeded in his mission by joining self-proclaimed liberators. The alliance between these members of the upper class was sufficient for the abolition of the Roman monarchy.

After this episode, the Roman Republic was established. The justification for the new regime was that a government led by a single individual, such as in a monarchy, led to terrible abuses of power, just like the rape of Lucretia.

The term "Republic" is derived from the Latin res publica, which means "public thing", "public affairs" or "community". This was the ideal of the Roman government: to be for the community. However, this concept was never fully put into practice as the upper class dominated both the government and society during this period.

REPUBLIC OF OFFICES

The Republican period in Rome was marked by the emergence of numerous political positions. These positions aimed to satisfy the desires of the patrician elite to actively participate in the government. This situation led to the appearance of several social conflicts at the time.

The presence of members of the upper class in the most important positions and in the political decisions of Rome fueled intense competition between these members and the wealthier plebeians, who were responsible for economic and military activities.

But the sources of conflict between patricians and plebeians in the early Republic were also economic. Poor plebeians were the most desperate ones for relief from the policies of the patricians during this period. With the population increase, this segment of the population needed more land for cultivation and sustenance. However, members of the elite dominated most of the properties and even made loans to the poor.

Due to the lack of farming land and the high interest rates on their debts, many plebeians decided to leave the sacred boundary of the city for a temporary settlement on a nearby hill. Furthermore, plebeians refused to serve in the militia's army of citizens. The secession worked. Roman defense became greatly compromised as they did not have a professional permanent army. This situation forced the patricians to concede, something they naturally did not like at all. Thus, they had to negotiate an agreement with the plebeians.

ROMAN LAW

According to local tradition, the agreement between the two parties led to the creation of the first written laws in Rome. The legal code came into effect after a Roman delegation visited Athens, where they studied how the Greek city had developed a written legal code. Despite this research, a long time was needed for the two Roman orders to reach a final agreement on the laws. This was because the pact needed, on the one hand, to protect the plebeians and, on the other hand, to ensure the status of the patricians.

The Law of the Twelve Tables, the oldest written code of Roman law, was promulgated between 451 and 449 BCE. Despite some advancements, the patricians took the opportunity to include the prohibition of marriage between patricians and plebeians. Nonetheless, it was very important for the plebeian class to have a written code of laws to prevent patrician magistrates, who judged most legal cases, from making arbitrary and unfair decisions based solely on personal interests.

In general, the Law of the Twelve Tables contained very practical and simple provisions, such as "If someone is summoned to court, they must appear" or "If a tree leans over a neighbor's land, its branches should be pruned to a height of more than fifteen feet". This set of rules demonstrated that the Romans had a strong interest in civil law. The criminal code, on the other hand, was never extensive. As a result, the courts did not have a vast set of rules to guide their verdicts.

POLITICAL SYSTEM

The Roman constitution included various elected officials and the Senate as a special body. The position of consul was the highest in the Republican period. Since the Republic was created to prevent a single individual from taking control of the government indefinitely, the consulship was established so that two leaders of the State would be elected to serve jointly. Their government term was one year, and reelection for consecutive mandates was prohibited.

The word consul meant "those who care for the community". It was a way to make it clear that the holders of the office should act on behalf of the interests of all Romans. The main duties of the consuls were to provide leadership in political and civil matters, as well as to command the army in times of war. The competition to attain this position was intense because holding it was a means of elevating the family's prestige for an extended period. Some families with only one consul among their ancestors would be called "noble".

The Senate, which persisted through all the centuries of Roman history, can be considered the most influential institution in the "Roman constitution". It is important to note that the Senate dates back to the monarchical period, and even the kings did not make important decisions alone, as it was a Roman tradition to always seek advice from friends and the elderly. Thus, the monarchs assembled a select group of experienced advisors who were called senators (Latin word for elders).

Therefore, the practice of a leader seeking advice continued throughout the republican period.

For most of its history, the Senate operated with about 300 members. General Sulla doubled that number with a significant reform in 81 BCE. Julius Caesar, in turn, increased the number to 900 in an effort to gain supporters during the civil war in the 40s BCE. In 13 BCE, Augustus reduced the Senate's membership again to 600.

According to historians, the Senate always included patricians and plebeians from the elite. Over time, candidates were required to possess a substantial amount of property in order to compete for the position of senator.

At the beginning of the Republic, senators were chosen by the consuls from men who had previously been elected as lower magistrates. Later on, the selection process was performed by the censors, who were special magistrates of high prestige. One of the greatest influences of the Senate was related to decisions regarding the declaration and conduction of wars. It is important to note that, during this time, Rome was almost constantly engaged in armed conflicts.

An important aspect is that, in the Republican period, the Senate did not have the power to vote on bills; it merely acted as an advisory body. In other words, it did not have the official right to veto or approve any decisions of the executive government but rather it had a status of respect and consideration among Roman citizens.

OFFICES

Obviously, the position of consul was considered the most important one in Rome. In sequence, the other positions followed a hierarchy of prestige. In order to reach the highest offices, though, one had to follow a career plan that typically began around the age of 20, often as an assistant to an official. The next step was to seek election as a quaestor, responsible for the financial administration of the State. The following position was that of an aedile, who was in charge of the difficult task of managing the maintenance of streets, sewers, temples, markets and other public works.

The next step within the hierarchy of the Roman power was to aim for victory in the annual election for the prestigious position of praetor, which was second in importance only to the consulship. Generally, praetors were responsible for administering justice and commanding war troops.

Thus, the power and prestige of these positions made them the center of dispute for public offices between patricians and plebeians. In 337 BCE, the pressure from the plebeian class forced the approval of a law that opened all offices evenly between the two orders.

The "Roman constitution" also had two special non-annual government positions: censor and dictator. The censor, who had to be a former consul, was responsible for the periodic counting of citizens and their properties so that taxes could be collected more fairly and Romans could be classified for military service. The position of dictator was occupied only in serious national emergencies when swift decision-making was necessary to ensure the State's well-being. Normally, the investiture of a dictator indicated that Rome had suffered a significant military loss and required extremely surgical action to prevent a disaster. The dictator had full powers, his decisions could not be questioned, but his tenure in the office was limited to a maximum of six months.

WAGE WORKERS

The entry into public service, however, was far from generating financial rewards for those holding office, as they did not receive a salary for their work. On the contrary, workers often had to spend some of their own money while performing their duties. Thus, it became clear that only those men with privileged financial conditions could engage in public office. They often obtained income through family properties or financial support from close friends.

Moreover, just like today, the costs of an election campaign were quite exacerbated. Candidates sometimes spent a significant amount of resources and even incurred enormous debts. Additionally, it was desirable that, after being elected, a government official used their own funds to finance public works such as roads, temples and aqueducts.

Although the beginning of the career offered only social status, as time went by, public officeholders began to profit financially, particularly due to the conquest of new territories. These officials gained the legal right to enrich themselves by collecting war booty when they held positions as commanders in successful conquest battles. Another way to gain profits - illicitly - was through accepting bribes while administering the provinces of the territories conquered by the Romans.

ASSEMBLIES

Decisions in Rome were made through voting in assemblies. In these outdoor events, the results of elections were defined, and new laws were approved. However, historians argue that such occasions were highly complex. Citizens – adults and free individuals – gathered after the convocation of a public official.

Debates occurred before the assemblies in a large gathering in which anyone – even non-citizens and women – could participate, but only male citizens had the right to speak. On the other hand, everyone could express their opinions through applause or booing for what was being said.

Nevertheless, at the beginning of the assembly itself, only proposals made by public officials could be voted on. It was also a moment to request amendments to the proposals.

At this time, the city of Rome had three different electoral assemblies: the Assembly of the Centuries, the Plebeian Tribal Assembly, and the Tribal Assembly of the People. However, the counting did not establish the "one man, one vote" rule. In the Assembly of the Centuries, for instance, citizens were divided into small groups according to the specific rules of each gathering. These groups were generally not of equivalent size. First, the members of each circle voted individually to determine what the group's single vote in the assembly would be. Thus, the sum of the single votes of the groups defined an assembly.

The major problem was that this procedure, apparently democratic, led to distortions in the election results. The richest and most powerful men composed smaller groups that had equal weight votes to much larger groups formed by poor citizens. Thus, the will of the absolute majority of people was rarely respected. To make matters worse, the voting began with the richest and proceeded to the less affluent people. As a result, members of the wealthier classes could vote as a block in the assembly, and by the time the vote reached the poorer citizens, the majority of votes had already been practically decided.

As for the electoral groups in the Plebeian Tribal Assembly, they were determined based on the location where citizens lived. This assembly was named after the Roman institution of tribes. At the time, there were up to 35 tribes, which were structured in geographical terms to give an advantage to wealthy landowners in rural areas. This assembly did not include the so-called patricians. Composed basically of plebeian voters, it conducted trials and various forms of public business. Especially in the early centuries of the Republican period, all proposals approved by the plebeians in these meetings were only considered recommendations, never laws. Thus, the aristocrats, who dominated the Roman government at that time, in many cases simply disregarded the recommendations made in these plebiscites.

Nonetheless, the plebeians began to revolt against this lack of consideration from the elite for their requests and desires. Therefore, the practice of secession was once again an important tool to pressure the Roman aristocracy. Repeated several times, this instrument of struggle forced the patricians to concede. A new rebellion movement in 287 BCE culminated in an agreement that turned decisions made in plebiscites into a source of official laws.

This change made the results of votes in the Plebeian Assembly change from mere recommendations to one of the main sources of legislation, even affecting the patricians themselves. The recognition of these plebiscites thus ended the conflict of orders between patricians and plebeians.

The Plebeian Tribal Assembly was responsible for electing, among others, the ten tribunes. These were special and powerful public officials dedicated to protecting the interests of the plebeian class. The power of the tribunes to obstruct the actions of other public officials and assemblies gave them enormous potential to influence the government of Rome. As a result, the office holders were often hated by members of the Roman elite, who, on numerous occasions, had their political wishes denied due to the tribunes' influence.

Subsequently, the Tribal Assembly also began to have expanded meetings with the participation of both patricians and plebeians. Meetings with this format were called the Tribal Assembly of the People. Such meetings served to elect, for example, the quaestors and could also enact laws and conduct trials considered of lesser importance.

Despite all attempts to reach a common ground, the struggle be-

Image of senator and his slaves: the Roman parliamentarian was a type of advisor to the consul

tween classes and powers generated many serious political conflicts during the Republic. Some contemporary historians believe that these conflicts were caused by the fact that various institutions could create equivalent laws or norms. Since Rome did not have a Supreme Court, it was not possible to resolve disputes over the validity of overlapping or conflicting laws.

Even with all this turmoil and movement, the wealthiest and highest-status Romans continued to dominate most of the Roman republican government.

To gain support from voters, candidates for public office in Rome financed fighting festivals between gladiators and battles involving animals brought from Africa.

3

WARS AND TERRITORIAL ADVANCE

THE ROMANS FACED HARD BATTLES TO SIGNIFICANTLY EXPAND THEIR DOMINION IN THE REPUBLICAN PERIOD

During its republican era, Rome waged wars that significantly expanded its territorial dominance. This expansion over lands previously ruled by other peoples was fundamental to the project of forming a real empire.

Besides bringing gains in land, this movement also generated profound changes in Roman society. After dominating various settlements, the Romans came into close contact with the way of life of other cultures. The clearest case was the interaction with the Greeks. This relationship even led to the creation of the first piece of Roman literature written in Latin.

Furthermore, the expansion caused a multitude of small Italian farmers to fall into poverty. This situation generated conflict among the elite members upon what to do with these needy countrymen. It was the forewarning of the end of the Republic.

FIRST COMBATS

The initial battles took place in the central region of Italy. The Romans achieved a significant triumph over Latin neighbors in 499 BCE shortly after the establishment of the republican regime. In the following hundred years, they engaged in intense conflicts against the Etruscans from the Veii region, north of the Tiber River. Victory came in the year 396 BCE and helped the Romans nearly double their territory. At that time, the Roman army was already considered the most powerful in the Mediterranean region. Its largest unit was the legion, composed, approximately, of 5,000 infantry soldiers. Each legion also had a rearguard of 300 cavalry troops, along with engineers responsible for supporting activities.

The legion was subdivided into smaller units, which were led by the so-called centurions. This was a way to ensure greater mobility of the army in case of necessary quick response to unexpected situations during combat. This formation left gaps between groups of a hundred men, allowing infantry soldiers to stay behind large shields while making effective use of spears to break the enemy's front line. Subsequently, they would wield their swords for the dreaded hand-to--hand combat.

According to historians, the swords used by the infantry were specially designed for striking opponents at very close range. Moreover, these men underwent rigorous training to endure the bloody confrontations. This high quality and intense preparation of the army aided Rome in its advances. By 220 BCE, imperialism was gaining stronger contours after all of Italy south of the Po River was under the control of the brave Romans.

After winning the arduous battles, Rome's strategy was to enslave the defeated peoples. When not doing so, they forced them to cede considerable stretches of land. Regarding conquered Italian peoples, the Romans did not require them to pay taxes but demanded from them military aid in battles. The new allies received a share of the spoils of war – such as slaves and land. In general terms, the Roman strategy was to incorporate former adversaries and thus make their wealth even greater over time. Given this scenario, experts on the subject emphasize that Roman imperialism was inclusive.

EXPANSION

Around 300 BCE, given this environment of progress, the Roman populational rate reached considerably high levels for the period. Approximately 150,000 people lived within the city's fortification walls alone. In order to meet the needs of this high demand, aqueducts were constructed to supply potable water to the city. Furthermore, the spoils of the victorious wars were used to finance an extensive housing construction project.

Outside the walls, approximately 750,000 Roman citizens and freedmen lived in different regions of Italy in lands taken from local peoples. However, the rural population faced economic challenges at the time due to the increase in the birth rate - making it impossible to support larger families – as well as the difficulty of maintaining a productive farm when many men were on very long and exhausting military campaigns. Furthermore, the large portions of land in the hands of a few contributed to the emergence of new underlying conflicts between wealthy and poor Romans.

FIRST PUNIC WAR

A battle, quite different at least, put Roman hegemony to the test between the years 280 and 275 BCE. The battle in the Greek city of Tarentum placed Rome against an army equipped with war elephants. The tactic was used by the mercenary general Pyrrhus to try to contain the almost inevitable adversary's advance into southern Italy.

Facing such a powerful enemy, Roman leaders convinced the assemblies to vote in favor of confronting this threat. Despite all the difficulties, after five years, Pyrrhus abandoned the war and returned to Greece. Hence, Rome gained complete control of southern Italy down to the Mediterranean coast at the end of the peninsula.

Before this expansion southward, the Romans were on the edge of the region dominated by Carthage, a very prosperous state located across the Mediterranean Sea where Tunisia is located today. In 800 BCE, the Phoenicians colonized Carthage, a region favorable for maritime trade and with fertile agricultural areas in its central part. Carthaginian trade extended throughout the western Mediterranean region, even reaching the island of Sicily, located in a narrow strip of sea at the tip of the Italian peninsula.

Carthage's prosperity generated avid interest from the Romans. The big problem was that they lacked naval experience for maritime combat, something the Carthaginians had in abundance. The citizens of Rome, in the 3rd century BCE, had practically no technological knowledge to build a warship and also lacked the necessary organization to form a powerful navy.

Therefore, a battle seemed unfeasible. Furthermore, there was no trace of enmity between these peoples to precipitate any kind of Roman action against Carthage. However, an insignificant episode changed this scenario and led to a destructive war that lasted for more than a century.

It all began in 264 BCE when a band of mercenaries in the city of Messina, in the far northeast of Sicily, were in a perilous situation after the military service for which they were hired ended in failure. Desperate, they decided to seek aid from both Carthage and Rome at the same time. The Roman Senate could not reach a consensus on what to do regarding the mercenaries' request for rescue. However, the patrician consul Appius Claudius Caudex persuaded the majority to vote for sending troops to the region of Sicily with the promise of excellent spoils. Thus, the dispatch of the army to Messina became Rome's first military expedition outside of Italy.

What no one expected was that Carthage would also send soldiers to that region. The encounter of the two armies ignited a battle between the forces of the two economic powers. As a result, the First Punic War erupted between 264 BCE and 241 BCE. Roman victory came from persistence. Prepared to sacrifice lives and spend a lot of money in the conflict, Rome lost 250,000 men and about five hundred newly built warships. A century later, the Greek historian Polybius considered the First Punic War the greatest war in history in terms of duration, intensity and scale of operations.

What is impressive is that, forced to fight at sea against a rival much better prepared for these conditions, Rome decided to develop its navy from scratch. They copied the ships and tactics of the adversary with the help of the Greeks and finally conquered Messina. Thus, the First Punic War ended in 241 BCE.

With the triumph, the Romans became masters of prosperous Sicily, a region full of ports and fields. The revenue coming from taxes the Romans received from the Sicilians was so high that in 238 BCE, two other Carthaginian colonies – the islands of Corsica and Sardinia – were also annexed by the empire.

SECOND PUNIC WAR

After the long war in the face of Carthage, the Romans decided to form alliances with communities located to the east of Spain to limit the enemy's influence in the region. Rome, nonetheless, had given assurances that it would not interfere on the south side of the Ebro River, which was under Carthaginian control.

Nevertheless, the authorities of a city called Saguntum, which was located precisely in that region, requested Roman assistance against Carthage. It is worth noting that Saguntum was a place with intense commercial activity in mineral and agricultural resources in Spain. Faced with this request, the Roman Senate simply ignored the previous promise not to intervene in the city and decided to provide assistance.

Perhaps the main reason for breaking the pact was the Roman belief that the Carthaginians were morally inferior barbarians. The Romans condemned them for the practice of sacrificing babies and children in national emergencies to regain the favor of the gods.

Thus, in 218 BCE, 23 years after the first conflict between Rome and Carthage, the Second Punic War began, ending only in 201 BCE. This new long conflict was even more wearing due to the fact that the Carthaginian general Hannibal Barca employed a daring tactic. He marched his troops and elephants through snow-covered mountain passageways in the Alps to invade Italy. In 216 BCE, 30,000 Romans were decimated in what became known as the Battle of Cannae.

Hannibal knew the extent of the Roman power and his strategy was to try to foment revolts in the Italian cities allied with Rome. He also correctly counted on an alliance with King Philip V of Macedonia in 215 BCE, forcing the Romans to fight in Greece. The Carthaginian general posed numerous difficulties for his opponents for 15 years. During this time, he marched through Italy, devastated parts of Roman territory and even threatened the sovereignty of the capital city itself.

However, Hannibal failed in his tactic to turn the Italian allies against Rome. On the contrary, they remained loyal, and the general had to conclude the guerrilla campaign in Italy to return to North Africa with his entire army in 203 BCE. In that same year, the Romans, under the command of General Scipio, launched a significant attack against Carthage. After long years, Hannibal would finally be definitively defeated in the Battle of Zama in 202 BCE.

To solidify their victory, the Romans imposed a punitive peace agreement on the Carthaginians. They made them sink their ships, pay very substantial war indemnities for fifty years and relinquish territories in Spain. Later on, Rome would still fight against Spanish indigenous peoples for control of the areas, but the profits the lands could generate for their owners - especially through mineral extraction - made the challenging endeavor worthwhile. These revenues were so considerable that they ensured the execution of high-cost public building projects in Rome.

After their success against Carthage, the Romans turned their attention to the conflict with the Gauls in northern Italy. This Celtic group was considered very dangerous, especially after they devastatingly plundered

Image of an old building in Sagunto: conflict in the region precipitated the Second Punic War

Rome in 387 BCE. It was, therefore, a preventive defense. By the end of the 3rd century BCE, the Romans already controlled the entire Po Valley – previously held by the Gauls – and, consequently, all of Italy up to the Alps.

THIRD PUNIC WAR

The year 146 BCE marked the annihilation of Carthage at the end of the Third Punic War (149 BCE to 146 BCE). The final conflict began when Carthage, having recovered from the indemnities imposed by Rome after the Second Punic War, attacked the neighboring Numidian king, Massinissa, a Roman ally. This time, the city was completely destroyed, and its territory became a province of the empire. The destruction of Carthage as an independent State was a response to the persistent demands of the Roman senator Marcus Pocius Cato, who feared even slight threats from that rival.

CHANGES

As a consequence of intense military and diplomatic activities, Roman relations with southern Italy, Sicily, Greece and Asia Minor became more effective, leading the Romans to have a deeper contact with Greek culture. This interaction profoundly influenced the development of art, architecture and literature in Roman culture. For instance, the first marble temple constructed in the capital city in 146 BCE was dedicated to Jupiter, following the Greek tradition of using this type of bright stone.

Literature also gained momentum through well-known and admired Greek models. Around 200 BCE, the first Roman story was written in the Greek language. As for the oldest literary piece written in Latin, a lengthy poem produced after the First Punic War, was an adaptation of the Odyssey, by Homer.

However social changes in the Roman Empire were also profound during this period. The upper class made considerable gains in the 2nd and 3rd centuries BCE, mainly by receiving war spoils.

Moreover, the creation of new provinces generated the need for a higher number of military and political leaders that could not be supplied by the traditional number of elected public officials. As a result, an increasing number of officials were granted extended powers to command troops and administer those provinces. However, since provincial governors operated under martial law, no one could prevent them from enriching themselves through corruption and extortion. Of course, not all of them were corrupt, and few of those who engaged in illegal activities were punished. One of the few examples was Verres, prosecuted by Cicero in 70 BCE for administrative crimes in Sicily.

POVERTY

At this time, the economic foundation was still agriculture. In these centuries, farmers worked on small pieces of land in inner Italy. In parallel, landowners represented the main source of soldiers for the army. Due to this situation, the Republic faced immense economic and social difficulties. During the wars, agricultural production was left highly vulnerable.

Before the occurrence of the Punic Wars, Rome maintained a military operation that followed normal Mediterranean patterns, that is, short scheduled military campaigns that did not interfere with agricultural activities. Seasonal combats allowed men to remain at home during the times of the year when they needed to sow and harvest crops, as well as oversee the mating and slaughter of animals. However, from the First Punic War onwards, campaigns became excessively lengthy and prevented these men from returning home periodically.

In many cases, women and children - especially the families of soldiers - died of starvation because they could not count on the male figure to provide for them. Other women resorted to prostitution in the cities of Italy to survive. Several farming families went into debt and had to sell their land. In turn, wealthy landowners could acquire these lands to create even larger plantations. These landowners expanded their holdings even further by illegally occupying public lands that Rome had confiscated from defeated peoples in Italy.

MIGRATION

Unable to farm and live decently, many people began to migrate to Rome. In the capital, men sought subordinate jobs. Women waited for occasional work in textile production. This army of desperate, food-seeking poor people swelled the city's population. This scenario turned the Roman political environment into a powder keg. Entire impoverished families were willing to support, through their votes, any politicians who promised to meet their most basic needs. In some way, the neediest had to be fed so as to minimize large-scale protests to the fullest.

Nonetheless, this policy generated much controversy. While some leaders believed it was the only possible solution to the looming problem, a significant portion of them disagreed vehemently but did not propose a better alternative. Thus, this policy persisted. Over the years, the number of those in need grew exponentially. Tens of thousands of people were part of this long list of those entitled to receive subsidies at no cost. To continue or not with this exponential expenditure generated increasing debate.

INTERNAL CONFLICTS

The total lack of consensus around assistance to the poor had devastating effects even on prominent family circles. Tiberius Gracchus and Gaius Gracchus came from one of the most distinguished high-class families in Rome: their mother Cornelia was the daughter of the legendary general Scipio Africanus. Tiberius was elected to the position of plebeian tribune in 133 BCE. Immediately, he made the Tribal Assembly of the Plebeians adopt reform laws aimed at redistributing public lands to Romans who did not own property. This measure was taken without the consultation and approval of the senators. The maneuver was legal – since the Senate could not block any measures –, but extremely unusual in the Roman tradition. He further challenged Roman political custom by simply ignoring the Senate on the issue of financing this agrarian reform proposal.

The reforms proposed by Tiberius to assist the dispossessed farmers obviously had a political root, as he needed to settle a debt with political rivals and aimed to become popular as an advocate of the most suffering people.

However, this momentum of Tiberius was violently halted. A former consul named Scipio Nasica organized a violent surprise attack against him. A group of senators and their clients murdered Tiberius and his associates with blows on Capitol Hill at the end of 133 BCE. In this bloody and non-republican way, this sad history of violence and assassination as a political tactic had begun in Rome.

Gaius Gracchus won the election for tribune in 123 BCE and, once again, in 122 BCE. Like his brother Tiberius, he initiated several reforms that meant a significant threat to the Roman elite. In addition to maintaining the agrarian reforms, he introduced laws that guaranteed grains to Roman citizens at prices subsidized by the state. He also managed to pass public work projects throughout Italy to employ the poor.

The most revolutionary of all his actions were his proposals to grant Roman citizenship to various Italians and to establish a jury tribunal for senators accused of corruption while holding government positions in the provinces. The citizenship proposal failed. However, the establishment of the tribunal for proceedings against senators generated enormous controversy because their cases would be reviewed by wealthy men. At the time, these citizens, known as equestrians, were more involved in business but still aspired to hold public office. Their entry into civil service, however, was often blocked by the senators.

Gaius's proposal to have the equestrians serve as jurors in senators' trials accused of illegality in the administration of the provinces marked their rise in Roman politics. This threat infuriated the Senate. In 121 BCE, the senators published a document authorizing the consul Opimius to employ military force within the city of Rome, where, according to tradition, not even public officials had such power. Gaius even tried to hire a bodyguard to protect himself against unexpected attacks. But, with no way out, he ordered one of his slaves to cut his throat in order to escape imminent detention and execution.

After the deaths of Tiberius and Gaius Gracchus, the members of the Roman upper class became increasingly divided. There was no possibility of reaching a consensus on whether or not to provide unrestricted assistance to the poor who were flooding the capital of the empire. Some political leaders still maintained their political alliances. Others simply aimed to openly promote their careers by pretending to be supporters of one side or the other. However, regardless of the stance adopted, the rift within the elite remained a major source of political turmoil and gratuitous violence in the final years of the Republic.

View of the Capitoline Hill, where Tiberius and his companions were allegedly murdered in 133 BCE

4

THE END OF THE REPUBLICAN ERA

CONFLICTS BETWEEN MEMBERS OF THE ROMAN ELITE AND INTERNAL REVOLTS DESTROYED THE REGIME AND MARKED A NEW ERA WITHIN THE EMPIRE

The lack of consensus regarding social policies made the republican regime in Rome unsustainable in the 1st century BCE. The deterioration process began during the consulships of Tiberius and Gaius Gracchus and lasted for about a hundred years. Civil wars during this period also helped accelerate this moment of degradation.

In addition, the Roman state began to face internal and external rebellions. At that time, around 70,000 slaves escaped from properties in the region of Sicily and joined forces to organize a revolt. The rebellion lasted for three years. It was also necessary to quell a foreign war with Jugurtha, a rebellious client king in North Africa. Finally, Gallic warriors launched several attacks in the northern regions of Italy.

The hostile environment paved the way for a new type of leader, someone without ties to the nobility but highly skilled in military leadership and with a better reputation for the position of consul. These new candidates for the position, despite lacking a distinguished family background, came to be called new men.

However, they had to overcome social prejudice to attain this position. This was made possible through noble gestures, such as generosity towards soldiers - who received spoils and had their needs met. In general, the common Roman soldier was poor. Thus, they saw in this new figure a commander they should consider their patron and to whom they owed obedience. This figure elicited more empathy than senators or members of assemblies. Hence, the patron-client system became a way for leaders to gain individual power instead of supporting the interests of the Roman community itself.

PRECURSOR

Gaius Marius (157 BCE to 86 BCE) was the one who most effectively put the reformed leadership idea into practice. Without noble roots, he would not have had the chance to reach a leadership position within the traditional Roman scene. His background would, at best, have taken him to a minor career in the Senate.

Nevertheless, a great and urgent need in Rome completely changed the game for him. By the end of the 2nd century BCE, the empire needed men with his characteristics and capabilities to lead an army to victory. Marius served masterfully in the North African War and gained notoriety. These battles had dragged on for a long time due to the incompetence of other generals. It was only with his arrival that the Romans could finally move toward victory.

Therefore, the general began to rise through some important ranks on the ladder of elective offices. His support for the interests of noble patrons and his marriage to a woman from a famous patrician family further helped him in his quest for the ultimate goal of becoming consul. A smart man, Gaius Marius knew how to use his good reputation and enviable history of military triumphs to win the elections for one of the consuls in 107 BCE.

His popularity was evident among the voters. So much so that his victories against the Northern Celts – a people who attempted to invade Italy on numerous occasions in the late 2nd century BCE – led to him being elected consul for six consecutive terms, an unprecedented achievement.

Gaius Marius still enjoyed the respect of the Senate, which honored him with Rome's ultimate military distinction. It was a rare recognition given only to generals who achieved outstanding triumphs. On the day of his appointment, the general paraded through the city streets in a military carriage and was acclaimed by the crowd.

However, even with his high popularity, Marius was never a consensus figure among the Roman elite. He was viewed as a threatening "new rich" man. His main support actually came from the equestrian order – the lower aristocratic class – and the common people. It is likely that the equestrians encouraged his entry into the nobility to prove the worth of this social class.

Gaius Marius's notoriety among the poorest citizens supposedly was, among other things, a reflection of the reforms he implemented regarding the requirements for a man to join Rome's army. While previously only men of means could enlist, at that time, proletarians had that right as well. This gave lower-class citizens the chance to aspire to the rewards of status and spoils that soldiers were entitled to in victorious campaigns. This was the greatest opportunity for these poor Romans to improve their lives somewhat. Not even the risk of being killed or seriously wounded deterred these men from going into battle.

In this period, the Roman State did not offer any form of rewards or pensions to former soldiers. Therefore, a good financial return depended on winning battles and on the generosity of the general. Since there was no more land in Italy to be distributed among veterans at that time, troops relied entirely on their share of the spoils. It is worth noting that the general had the right to keep most of the plunder for themselves. That is why proletarian troops felt immense gratitude when their leader was generous in distributing the spoils.

Faced with Gaius Marius's behavior, the loyalty of the soldiers was increasingly directed towards their generals and not necessarily towards the State. Thus, the Roman army began to behave like a legion of clients, dutifully following their leaders and placing State interests second.

This period marked a reorganization of the Roman army, with the use of new tactics. Legions now consisted of ten units, each with 480 men. Each unit had six centuries of 80 men commanded by a centurion. During this time, the equipment, once composed of various types, also became more uniform.

The main infantry carried spears, swords and large shields. Marus designed the use of heavy spears to bend after impacting the enemy's shield, which prevented its movement and made it easier to

In open-car ceremonies of military honor, it was quite common for the honored general to have a slave behind him, warning: "Look behind and remember you are mortal". This practice was a way to prevent pride and fame from going to one's head kill. Afterward, Roman soldiers would attack the adversary and use swords in individual combat.

SOCIAL WAR

While Gaius Marius's army paved the way for significant victories, it also brought about problems. His troops became a source of political power for unscrupulous commanders who destabilized the Republic politically. Marius, however, was too attached to tradition to use his army to retain his own career. With this stance, he eventually lost political significance after the year 100 BCE.

At the beginning of the 1st century BCE, the growing crisis in the relationship between the capital and its Italian allies escalated into a war. Roman tradition says that allies would typically share the spoils of military triumphs. Yet, they were not Roman citizens and lacked the right to influence domestic or international policy decisions. This situation left them dissatisfied as they witnessed the Republic's wealth increase significantly. The Italians desired a much more equitable distribution.

The dissatisfaction among the allies reached an unacceptable level in 91 BCE when violence erupted within the Roman Republic during the Social War. The internal conflict - named Social War because the Latin word for "ally" is socius - lasted for four years.

The Italians joined forces to establish a new republic, which was called Italy. They decided to form a confederation – composed of the Picentes, Lucanians, Marsi, Samnites, Apulians, Etruscans and Umbrians - to fight against Rome. They even minted their own currency and established their Senate. The conflict featured many battles. The first ones were won by the Italians. However, when Lucius Cornelius Sulla assumed command of the Roman army in 90 BCE, the tide turned. From then on, Rome crushed the Samnites. Some sources estimate that approximately 300,000 Italians were killed in battle.

At the end of the war, Rome theoretically emerged victorious. However, the Italians achieved some of their objectives. In order to ensure a peaceful environment, Rome decided to grant citizenship to the Allies, which was the reason for their rebellion in the first place. From that moment on, free-born people in Italy, south of the River Po, enjoyed the privileges of Roman citizenship. One of these privileges – probably the most important for them – included the right to vote in assemblies.

MITHRIDATIC WARS

The bloody Social War was only a precursor to the difficulties that Rome would face. A rebellion erupted in Asia Minor shook the fragile republican structure even more. The King of Pontus, Mithridates VI, led a revolt primarily due to the arbitrary way taxes were collected in that region.

It is worth observing that Roman officials did not collect these taxes directly. The capital would hold a kind of auction among private entrepreneurs to determine who would do the job. The highest bidder would win the contract and could keep any extra money collected. Consequently, tax collectors would exert brutal pressure on the locals to maximize their profits.

Mithridates achieved immediate success in his military action. A surprise attack resulted in the massacre of tens of thousands in a single day. It triggered the First Mithridatic War, which took place between 88 BCE and 85 BCE. In total, it took three wars for Rome, with extreme difficulty, to finally repel the threat posed by the King of Pontus.

CIVIL WAR

Lucius Cornelius Sulla emerged from the Social and Mithridatic Wars with a high standing. Thanks to his successful command of the Roman army, this noble Roman - hailing from a declining patrician family - won the election for the consulship in 88 BCE. Faced with Sulla's growing power, his former subordinate, Marius conspired to remove him from office.

That was when Lucius Cornelius Sulla took a bold step. Taking advantage of his army of clients, he marched with his soldiers against Rome, sparking a civil war. By capturing Rome with troops composed of Roman citizens, Sulla brutally killed or exiled political opponents. After that, he led his soldiers on a military campaign in Asia Minor.

After Sulla left Italy, Gaius Marius and his allies regained control of Rome. Sulla's violence was tackled with more violence from then on. The Roman territory was immersed in a sea of hatred and bloodshed. Marius died shortly thereafter, but his followers retained power until 83 BCE when Sulla returned from Asia Minor with a significant victory under his belt.

A new civil war erupted as Sulla's opponents joined forces with other Italians to combat their common enemy. According to the historian Thomas R. Martin, "the culminating battle of the war occurred at the end of 82 BCE at the Colline Gate of Rome". The Samnite general reportedly incited his men against Sulla, saying, "The final day is near for the Romans! These wolves who have ravaged the freedom of the Italian peoples will never disappear until we cut down the forest that serves as their refuge". However, despite the excitement, the Samnites lost the battle and the war. They were annihilated and their territory fell into the hands of Sulla and his supporters.

He even terrorized his enemies in Rome using a martial law measure called "proscription". The tactic involved publishing a list of names of individuals accused of treason. Any citizen could hunt down and kill these individuals without the need for any prior trial. The property of the proscribed was confiscated and distributed to the killers. Sulla's allies then began adding to this macabre list the names of innocent men who owned plenty of land. Thus, they had the perfect pretext to punish "supposed traitors" and seize their valuable and coveted properties.

Realizing that his health was deteriorating, Sulla retired from public life in 79 BCE and died the following year.

POMPEY

The new model of Roman leadership left by Sulla created successors. Men who sought power for themselves while proclaiming to be working for the State. Gnaeus Pompeius (106 BCE to 48 BCE) was the first leader in this wave. Still very young, at only 23 years old, Pompey (as he is known in English) is said to have assembled, according to tradition, a private army of his father's clients in Italy to join Sulla in the campaign to regain control of the capital in 83 BCE. The young man achieved the feat of defeating Sulla's remaining enemies who had fled to Sicily and North Africa. This episode earned him the honor of celebrating a triumph, an unusual achievement for younger men, especially for someone who had never held a public office.

The continuation of his career showed that he did not care much about Roman traditions. After Sulla left the scene, he seized power for himself. He helped suppress a rebellion in Spain and a highly significant slave revolt in Italy led by the gladiator Spartacus. As a result of his military triumphs, he demanded and was elected consul in 70 BCE, long before reaching the legal age of 42 years.

VICTORY OVER PIRATES

In the year 67 BCE, Pompey was elected to be a commander with extensive powers to combat over a thousand pirate ships that were plaguing the routes of the Mediterranean Sea. The Roman consul commanded 500 ships, 120 thousand men and 5,000 horses.

His strategy in this battle was quite clever. He divided the Mediterranean into 13 regions, because if he tried to attack in one single area, the pirates would have time to react. His strategy worked. The opponents could not counter the Roman offensive. They even tried to flee to the region of Sicily but, within just 40 days, the thieves threatening the maritime trade of the Roman Empire were already dispersed. Around 20 thousand of them were quickly captured.

ACHIEVEMENTS AND PROBLEMS

Pompey's success brought him glory. He was even compared to Alexander the Great. Hence, he was named Magnus, which earned him the title "Pompey the Great." He boasted of significantly increasing Rome's provincial revenues and distributed money to the soldiers, equivalent to 12 years' worth of pay, just from their share of the spoils.

When conquering a territory, he did not consult the Senate on the political arrangements to follow. He behaved more like an independent king than a major representative of the Republic.

However, Pompey's successes also brought him difficulties. Rival members of the Roman higher class were resentful and fearful. Among them were Marcus Licinius Crassus - who led the victory against Spartacus - and the young Julius Caesar (100 BCE to 44 BCE). To garner support against Pompey, they decided to help the less fortunate and became popular leaders.

The population of Rome was very large and a significant portion of it lived crowded into buildings no better than slums. Finding employment was challenging. Many survived on the grain distributions provided by the central government. It was dangerous to walk in the streets as the city lacked an established police force. The economic situation was also unfavorable and property prices were clearly decreasing.

TRIUMVIRATE

In the year 62 BCE, when Pompey returned to Rome after his

victory in the Mediterranean, the political leaders decided to refuse support for his territorial arrangements and to authorize the distribution of land as rewards to war veterans. This retaliation was fueled by envy of his fame. This episode forced Pompey to form a political alliance with Crassus and Julius Caesar. Thus, the First Triumvirate - a union of three men - was formed.

Caesar was elected consul in 59 BCE and received an expanded special command in Gaul. Crassus, on the other hand, secured financial opportunities for Roman tax collectors in Asia Minor, gaining political importance and more financial resources.

The triumvirates - later reformed - were political inventions that ignored the Roman constitution. Their only exclusive purpose was to benefit their members. To sustain this structure, the members of the Triple Union began to enter into politically motivated marriages among themselves. In 59 BCE, Julius Caesar forced his daughter, Julia, to marry Pompey. She was already engaged to another man, but Pompey himself reassured the jilted fiancé by marrying him to his own daughter. What began as a purely politically motivated arrangement between Pompey and Julia turned into an intense passion. This relationship helped prevent Pompey from immediately severing his political alliance with Caesar. However, in 54 BCE, when Julia died during childbirth along with the child she was carrying, the bond between the leaders was definitely broken.

JULIUS CAESAR X POMPEY

Consul in Gaul (modern-day France) from 58 BCE, Caesar became Pompey's greatest rival and decided to struggle for the highest office in Rome. He began formulating his strategy during the Gallic Wars. After defeating the Gauls, Julius Caesar crossed the Rubicon, a river that separates Italy from Gaul, heading toward Rome. The Senate already viewed him as a real threat and a future dictator.

With no alternative before his rival, Pompey faced enemy troops in Italy, Spain and the Balkans. Caesar defeated him on all three occasions. Finally, at Pharsalus - in northern Greece - came Pompey's definitive defeat, despite having a well-armed cavalry. Caesar's armies outmaneuvered their opponents, killing 6 thousand adversaries and capturing another 24 thousand men. Pompey, after 34 years of military invincibility and at the age of 59, had to flee. He set sail for Egypt.

As Egyptian king, Ptolemy was only 10 years old and the local government was administered by a council consisting of Potinus, Theodotus and Achillas. The trio feared Caesar and plotted a trap for Pompey. Achillas summoned the tribune Septimius and the centurion Salvius. The three men were given Pompey's boat and he was assassinated. His head was severed and brought to Julius Caesar, who, a decade later, was appointed dictator of Rome (48 BCE).

CAESAR AND CLEOPATRA

After defeating Pompey, the leader traveled to Egypt to collect a sum of money the Egyptian government owed to the Roman treasury since the reign of Cleopatra's father. However, political affairs made way for the famous romance between Julius Caesar and Cleopatra.

King Ptolemy XIII - Cleopatra's brother -, upon learning of their affair, incited the people of Alexandria to revolt against the Romans. The Roman army was surrounded and besieged in the palace. Reinforcements to aid Caesar arrived only months later but managed to defeat Ptolemy's allies. The young pharaoh was found dead by drowning in the Nile River. In keeping with tradition, Cleopatra married her last surviving brother, Ptolemy XIV.

Yet, the romance between Caesar and Cleopatra was evident to all. They reportedly sailed together on the Nile for two months, as lovers. However, historians emphasize that the primary reason for Caesar's extended stay in Egypt was different: as April was the month of the Egyptian wheat harvest, he took the opportunity to stock his ships with the cereal. It is worth noting that a significant portion of the wheat consumed in Rome came from Egypt.

Julius Caesar never married Cleopatra. That is because he was already married to Calpurnia, a Roman woman with whom he never had children.

CAESAR'S GOVERNMENT

In 47 BCE, in the month of July, Cleopatra gave birth to a son. He was named Ptolemy XV but he became known as Caesarion.

Caesar acknowledged paternity. However, currently, many question who the true father of the child was. According to some contemporary historians, Cleopatra hoped that her son would not only inherit the kingdom of Egypt but also Julius Caesar's legacy. If this were to happen, Caesarion would become the ruler of an empire comparable to that of Alexander the Great of Macedonia.

The birth of Cleopatra's son was quite convenient for Caesar. As the father of the heir to the Egyptian throne, he could ensure the shipment of Egyptian wheat to Roman territory without significant expenses. In 44 BCE, Caesar removed any time limits on his dictatorship. So much so that his coins bore the inscription "dictator in perpetuity". Since there was a strong aversion to monarchy in Rome, he insisted on saying:

"I am not a king, I am Caesar". But the distinction he made was, in practice, insignificant. As a dictator, he personally controlled the government.

Elections for public offices continued, but Caesar was the one determining the outcomes by recommending candidates to the assemblies, which were dominated by his supporters. And naturally, his "recommendations" were immediately obeyed. He was ambitious in his government. He reduced debts moderately, initiating a vast program of public works - including the construction of libraries - establishing colonies for veterans in Italy and extending citizenship to non-Romans. Caesar also reformed the calendar, introducing a year of 365 days. This system was based on an ancient Egyptian calendar and forms the basis of the modern calendar.

DOWNFALL

This leader ruled Rome as he pleased. He forced senators to approve bills they had not read. He increased the number of members in the Senate to appoint friends to the new positions. He still harbored dreams of conquering the Parthian Empire (the region between the Aral Sea and the Caspian Sea) so as to create a new world monarchy. However, on the eve of launching another military campaign, he was attacked by conspirators. On March 15, 44 BCE, he was assassinated by 60 senators, who accused him of wishing to be king, which would mean the end of the Republic and the return of monarchy. He was allegedly stabbed 23 times on the stairs of the Senate.

On the very unusual fact of having been honored for a great military victory at just 23 years old – since great generals only received honors at older ages –, Pompey reportedly told Sulla: "More men worship the rising than the setting sun".

> Julius Caesar was more benevolent towards his enemies than other leaders. He was proud of his clemency and regarded his former adversaries as his clients. As a reward, Caesar received unprecedented honors, such as a golden seat in the Senate and the renaming of the seventh month of the year (Julius, giving rise to July).

History says that the group was led by Marcus Julius Brutus, his adopted son. Julius Caesar tried to defend himself, covering himself with a toga. Upon seeing Brutus, he reportedly uttered his famous last words: "You too, Brutus". What the conspirators could not anticipate was that Caesar's assassination would not bring the republican system back but would lead to a new civil war and the necessary conditions for the rise of a real monarchy.

After the episode, Cleopatra was surprised to learn that Caesar's will designated his nephew Octavian, not Caesarion, as his principal heir. The most famous political assassination of antiquity ended the controversial dictator's life. Nonetheless, the name "Caesar" continued to be used for many years as a title for future Roman emperors.

5

THE RISE OF THE ROMAN EMPIRE

AFTER BLOODSHED IN COUNTLESS WARS, A RENOVATED MONARCHIC GOVERNMENT SYSTEM DEVELOPED BY CAESAR AUGUSTUS REAPPEARS IN 27 BCE

The assassination of Julius Caesar, in 44 BCE would mark the sad end of the Republic and also a new stage in Roman history. In 27 BCE, the monarchical system was back, even though it was not called that way. In that year, Octavian had already defeated all his rivals and adopted the name Augustus - claiming to be improving the Republic. Contemporary historians unanimously say it was a disguised monarchy and assert that such rulers were, in reality, emperors.

Regardless of that, the great merit of the new system was to have put an end to decades of civil war. The concentration of power in the hands of a sovereign man brought back values such as loyalty to the ruler and his family. Octavian, in turn, maintained important and already established institutions in the Roman environment - such as the Senate, the ladder of offices, assemblies and tribunals. Meanwhile, he acted as an emperor without claiming the privileges of such a position.

CONFLICTS

After Julius Caesar's death, the battle for the tyrant's vacancy was not peaceful. More civil wars marked the moment. The initial contenders were Lepidus and Mark Antony - two experienced generals - along with Octavian, Caesar's great-nephew, who was only 19 years old. The latter was a novice in the military, whose new identity as Caesar's son earned him the loyalty of those soldiers who had adored the dictator.

With the support of his adoptive father's veteran soldiers, who were awaiting rewards for the deceased general, Octavian was studying in Greece. So, he sent them to fight against Mark Antony in Northern Italy. After an initial triumph, he marched with his men to the capital. There, he demanded to be elected consul, even though he had no experience in public office. Rather fearful, the senators granted Octavian the position. This was undoubtedly the biggest exception to the tradition of the ladder of offices.

Subsequently, Octavian decided to join forces with Mark Antony and Lepidus to face a new civil war against their enemies in Italy. They won the battle and, in November 43 BCE, formed a new Triumvirate - a government of three leaders. They forced the Senate to recognize the alliance as an official emergency measure for the reconstruction of the State. Together, they triumphed over the "Liberators" army in 42 BCE at the Battle of Philippi, northern Greece. Nonetheless, Octavian and Mark Antony conspired against each other to relegate Lepidus to a lesser position. He became the governor of North Africa but lost any decision-making power over Roman affairs.

Therefore, Mark Antony and Octavian began to share Roman control. The former held territories in the Eastern Mediterranean - including the lands of Egypt. The latter controlled Italy and the Western territories. However, over time, their relationship became more hostile.

Antony joined forces with the Queen of Egypt, Cleopatra VII. Cleverly, she turned the relationship into more than an alliance: they had a romantic relationship. In response, Octavian gathered the Romans and claimed that his rival had plans to make Cleopatra their foreign ruler. Furthermore, he also turned the inhabitants of Italy and the western provinces into clients, forcing them to swear loyalty to him in 32 BCE. Thus, Octavian managed to win a naval war against Cleopatra and Antony off the coast of Actium in Northwestern Greece on 31 BCE. The defeated lovers decided to flee to Egyptian soil, where they reportedly committed suicide a year later. Octavian took control of the richly endowed kingdom of Egypt. Wealthy and ruling a powerful army, he became the undisputed and by far the most prosperous leader of the time.

RESTORATION OF THE REPUBLIC?

After his victory, Octavian - the leader of an army of clients - distributed land to veteran soldiers to create communities loyal to him. In the year 27 BCE, he made a public announcement that he was restoring the

Historians state that Cleopatra VII decided to end her own life in a very unusual way. She would have let herself be bitten by a poisonous snake, symbol of royal authority.

Republic. He also stated that it would be the task of the Senate and the Roman people to decide how the government should be preserved from that moment on. However, the senators recognized that Octavian owned overwhelming power and begged him to continue to steer the situation to protect the State. In doing so, they granted him the honorary name of Augustus - which meant "favored by the gods". At the time, Octavian considered changing his name to Romulus, which would have positioned him as a second founder of Rome. Nevertheless, he pondered that the title of king was dangerous in that political moment.

The reality is that the form of government established by Augustus is now called the principate, derived from his title of princeps - which means "the first". The choice of the designation "first man" was a brilliant move. In the republican period, such an honorary designation was given to the highest status senator, to whom other members of the Senate turned for guidance. Hence, Augustus implicitly indicated that he was continuing one of the most valued republican traditions.

To reinforce the idea that he was simply continuing the Republic, he kept alive the discourse that he only continued as a political leader due to the insistence of the senators. He also obliged them to periodically approve the granting of powers of consul and tribune even without exercising these functions. This was the way Augustus managed to maintain himself as a kind of concealed emperor. Caesar Augustus also decided to continue with the traditional ceremony. He dressed like a normal citizen and not like a monarch.

The government structure in the years after 27 BCE helped maintain the republican appearance. The annual elections of consuls and other offices, the existence of the Senate and the approval of legislation in the Assemblies are some good examples of practices that ensured this image. This was because Augustus's control was exercised in the army and the public treasury. These institutions were reconfigured intending to ensure the maintenance of power. The army ceased to be a citizen militia to become a permanent force. Imperial revenue was used to ensure soldiers' salaries and retirement benefits. To cover additional costs, Augustus instituted an inheritance tax. Direct taxation of citizens, something quite rare, disproportionately affected the wealthy, which caused discontent.

HOUSE IN ORDER

Over time, Caesar Augustus decided to focus his attention on the security of the Empire's perimeter. In general, most of the army was tasked with overseeing the provinces in order to prevent internal rebellions and diverse foreign invasions.

Starting in 27 BCE, the Roman leader began to station soldiers in the capital itself. These men were called praetorians because of their original function of being stationed as bodyguards near the tent (praetorium) of a commander in the field. These troops composed the main imperial guard, although the emperor also relied on a small group of German mercenaries - loyal only to him - for personal protection. The existence of these groups was a way to demonstrate that the ruler's superiority lay in the threat of force, not just in supposed moral authority alone.

IMAGE

Portraying the emperor figure as a successful leader and generous patron was of fundamental importance to ensure the stability of that political system. To convey this concept, Augustus used coins as a means of political propaganda. On these coins, one could read messages proclaiming him as the "restorer of liberty". Others made reference to significant works he had envisioned.

Augustus, in fact, emphasized another Roman tradition: as a wealthy man, he used his own money to build important public structures. It is important to note that the emperor inherited a massive fortune from Julius Caesar, and he multiplied his earnings through the spoils of war and conquests, especially in Egypt. His architectural projects not only ensured improvements in public facilities but also conveyed the message to the people that their emperor was quite generous.

The new forum - a public square next to the old Roman Forum - was entirely funded by Augustus. According to historian Thomas R. Martin, "the work in the city center fully illustrates his skill in sending clear messages to the masses through stones and statues". The Forum of Augus-

AUGUSTUS'S ARMY SUFFERS DEFEAT IN GERMANY

Always in obedience to their leader, the soldiers accepted the challenges proposed without hesitation. Gratitude for the patron moved that group of men heading to very dangerous tasks.

In one of them, in the year 9 A.D., Augustus designated the military forces of Rome for an expedition that aimed to expand domination to present-day Germany. However, the mission's three legions were exterminated in an ambush in the Teutoburg Forest. The Roman army retreated and did not achieve its great objective.

The story tells that Augustus was in despair, as he feared a series of rebellions and attacks. Furthermore, in his assessment, damages for the loss of so many men at war could be overwhelming. According to the Latin writer Gaius Suetonius, at this time, Augustus stopped shaving and cutting his hair for months. He wandered around his residence in Rome and banged his head at a door while shouting at the expedition's dead commander:

"Quintilius Varus, return my legions".

tus was formally opened in 2 BCE and included a temple for Mars (the Roman god of war) and Venus (the goddess of love), who the emperor claimed as his divine ancestor. The sanctuary was built as a thanksgiving to the deities for his triumph over the forces of Caesar's assassins. It displayed Julius Caesar's sword as a memorial to his adoptive father.

Augustus's concern for his image is evident even in his choice of residence. The Roman emperor made sure to build his personal residence on Palatine Hill, where he lived modestly. Such a fact, clearly, was widely publicized in order to portray him as an ordinary citizen. In contrast, the emperors who succeeded him lacked this political astuteness and constructed gigantic palaces on the same hill with panoramic views of the Circus Maximus, the location of chariot races - one of Rome's favorite public entertainments.

During his reign, Augustus also prepared a lengthy document. He wanted the letter, which described all his achievements as a ruler, to be disseminated everywhere after his death. In it, Augustus states in the first person that his career was firmly rooted in the traditions of the Republic.

In general, historians diverge upon the real intentions of Caesar Augustus. While some categorize him as a ruthless and unscrupulous emperor whose sole aim was to seize power by suppressing the freedom of the Republic, others consider him a well-intentioned reformer who found a way to overcome an anarchic scenario in a disguised monarchy.

Despite suffering from many illnesses during his life, he governed Rome until his death in 14 CE at the age of 75. It was a total of 41 years of a long reign. As the historian Tacitus observed a century later, Augustus lived so long that, by the time he died, "hardly anyone who had seen the Republic was still alive". However, even the younger generations could recognize that the emperor brought rare stability to Roman society, which helped transform it into the great empire of the era.

JULIO-CLAUDIAN DYNASTY

Before his death, Augustus carefully planned the power succession in Rome. Since he had no natural heir, he adopted Tiberius, the adult son of his wife Livia from her previous marriage. Tiberius had a distinguished military record. Caesar then informed the Senate that the army wanted this adopted son to be in the line of succession.

The senators were quite prudent in confirming Augustus's choice regarding the succession after the first emperor's death. Members of Caesar's family - known as the Julio-Claudians due to the names of the family lines of Augustus (Julians) and Tiberius (Claudians) - continued to hold the position of "first man" for the next 50 years with the Senate's approval. Tiberius took office and remained emperor for 23 years until 37 CE. His long reign was only made possible due to his qualifications: in addition to the familial

Image of the Forum of Augustus, a project entirely funded by the emperor

connection with his predecessor, his brilliant military background earned him the utmost respect of the entire Roman army.

However, political success caused personal loss. To become Caesar's successor, he had to strengthen family ties. Augustus forced Tiberius to divorce his wife, Vipsania, in order to marry his daughter, Julia. It was a strictly political and extremely unhappy marriage because he still loved his ex-wife deeply. Tiberius never fully recovered from the sadness. He spent the last decade of his life secluded in a palace on the island of Capri, near Naples, and never returned to Rome.

Despite having a reputation for being disliked and unpopular, Tiberius managed to provide the nation with a peaceful period of transition. That was what the Empire needed to establish a common ground between the emperor and the elite, which had been discontented during the time of Caesar Augustus. While ruling as a monarch, he needed the cooperation of the upper class in public administration positions, army commanders and provincial leaders. As long as this relationship was good, the government and the elite could enjoy respect and status. The wealthier classes continued to relish the prestige of roles like consuls, praetors and senators. Meanwhile, the emperors could make their superior status clear by deciding who would occupy these positions. Thus, the Assemblies soon became mere automatic authorizations for the emperor's desires. Hence, these meetings lost much of their former power.

In 23 CE, Tiberius decided to build a permanent camp in the city for the Praetorian Guard. This facilitated the use of these soldiers to support him if forceful action was necessary. He reportedly died in his bed from natural causes. However, a rumor spread throughout the Empire said that he had been smothered. In fact, news of his death was enthusiastically celebrated by many people.

CALIGULA

Gaius was the successor to Tiberius in the Julio-Claudian dynasty. Better known as Caligula (12 to 41 CE), he harbored a deadly flaw in politics: an excessive love for power. Furthermore, he had not built a solid military career like other Roman leaders. The truth is that Tiberius chose him as his successor because he was the great-grandson of Caesar Augustus's sister.

Despite lacking such attributes, Gaius could have achieved success in his endeavor because, at the beginning of his reign, he enjoyed considerable popularity among the people. He also had an understanding of military matters, despite the lack of practical experience.

However, upon receiving unlimited power, Caligula showed that he did not possess a leadership personality. In reality, he carried in his heart the desire to satisfy his personal interests. Tiberius' successor ruled ruthlessly, using violence to address various problems. He also squandered public funds for his own pleasure. To fill the hole he created in the treasury, he imposed new taxes on sales in all sectors. Gaius taxed even quick meals on the street and sexual acts performed by prostitutes.

Vain, he even exaggerated in his public conduct, engaging in simulated gladiatorial battles and making appearances on stages as a singer, actor and even dressed as a woman. Caligula is also said to have had sexual relationships with his own sisters. The emperor's behavior exceeded all limits. In 41 CE, to put an end to his debauchery, two soldiers from the Praetorian Guard killed him in revenge for the insults directed at them.

MENACE TO DYNASTY

The Julio-Claudian period was in jeopardy after the assassination of Caligula since he had no children, and his violent behavior had greatly frightened the population of Rome. Upon hearing news of the homicide, a faction of senators moved to restore the original Republic. However, this attempt was thwarted by the Praetorian Guard, who wanted the emperors to continue as their patrons. The soldiers literally dragged Claudius – a relative of Augustus's who showed no apparent capacity to govern – to the camp and, by force, made the Senate proclaim him the new sovereign.

Claudius, at the age of 50, took power and demonstrated competence in Roman leadership. He established an essential precedent for the government of the Empire by enlisting men from the province of Transalpine Gaul – Southeastern France – into the Senate for the first time. This modification paved the way for the importance of having provinces as clients of the emperors, whose function was to help maintain the Empire's peace and prosperity. The ruler also allowed the employment of freed slaves in powerful administrative positions, expecting their loyalty.

What Claudius did not anticipate was the betrayal of his own wife, Agrippina, who poisoned him in 54 CE. She wanted Nero (37 to 68 CE) – the adolescent son of a previous husband – to become emperor instead of Claudius's own son. Agrippina achieved her goal, and in that same year, Nero ascended the throne. The new emperor had a difficult personality and also fell into the dangerous traps provided by absolute power. He lacked proper military training and was not adequately prepared to govern an Empire.

What Nero had in abundance was a passion for music and the dramatic arts. Thus, the luxurious public festivals he organized and the money distributed to the masses kept his popularity soaring. Nero spent enormous sums solely on his pleasures. In order to obtain more money, he would often fabricate accusations of treason against wealthy citizens. Thus, he was able to confiscate their properties.

Faced with such a problematic and controversial government, outraged provincial commanders supported rebellions against him. Senators also instigated an uprising. Nero's downfall came when one of the commanders of the Praetorians bribed them to desert the emperor. In 68 CE, fearing arrest and execution, he had no other choice: he asked a servant to cut his throat. Before dying, he is said to have exclaimed, "Qualis artifex pereo!" which translates to "What an artist dies in me!", in English.

NEW DYNASTY

Nero's death left Rome without a successor as he had no children. The end of the Julio-Claudian dynasty was decreed. As a result, in 68 CE, a civil war erupted among those interested in seizing power. The winner of the battle for the Roman emperor's position was the general Vespasian. Therefore, in 69 CE, he established his family – the Flavians – as the new dynasty.

To legitimize the new regime, Vespasian compelled the Senate to recognize him as ruler with a detailed declaration of the powers he was to have. It was officially transformed into law. In order to foster loyalty in the provinces, he encouraged members of the local elites to participate in the imperial cult. These celebrations included the sacrifice of animals to the gods for the emperor's well-being and, in some cases, the worship of the emperor himself. The veneration of leaders as true divinities seemed normal to residents of the provinces, who had been honoring local kings in this way for centuries, dating back to the time of Alexander the Great in the 4th century BCE.

As the worship of the emperor was already established in the eastern part of the Empire, Vespasian sought to strengthen the idea among the peoples of the provinces in Spain, Southern France and North Africa. However, the concept did not gain traction among the inhabitants of

Italy. In fact, Italians were generally disdainful of the imperial cult.

During a period of stability, Vespasian ruled sovereignly until his death in 79 CE. He laid the foundation for the continuity of the emerging new dynasty.

CONTINUITY

The Flavian dynasty continued with Vespasian's sons, Titus and Domitian. However, both of them inherited profound problems. Firstly, they needed to improve the lives of the people to prevent disorder. Secondly, they had to take great care in defending themselves against invasions from other peoples on the borders.

Titus gained fame in 70 CE by defeating a four-year-long Jewish rebellion in what is now Israel and by capturing Jerusalem. The Temple of Jerusalem, where Jewish rituals took place, was destroyed in the attack and was never rebuilt. During his brief reign (79 to 81 CE), Titus also assisted communities affected by the volcanic eruption at Mount Vesuvius in 79 CE.

In addition to these emergency actions, Titus was also an entertainment provider for the Roman masses. He completed the Colosseum in 80 CE, equipping the structure with enormous awnings to provide shade for the crowds. Titus died the following year of natural causes.

His brother Domitian assumed power in 81 CE and remained in office until 96 CE. He led the army to combat Germanic invaders, from the North to the areas along the Rhine and Danube rivers. It was the beginning of dangerous border battles that would intensify over the years. However, what ultimately led to Domitian's downfall was his arrogance. Historian Suetonius reported that Domitian would often declare, when communicating his wishes either in person or in writing, "Our Master and God, myself, orders you to do this". He also expanded his palace on the Palatine Hill to over 344,000 square feet. His behavior generated discontent. After a conspiracy emerged within his own household, Domitian was assassinated on September 18, 96 CE.

GOLDEN AGE

During this period, the assassination of an emperor no longer caused so much political turmoil. It was merely a reason to begin the search for a new name that would please the army.

The five following emperors established a period of relative peace in Rome. This era became known as the political Golden Age of the Empire because these rulers managed to provide stability for nearly a century. Nerva ruled from 96 to 98 CE; Trajan stayed in power from 98 to 117; Hadrian was emperor from 117 to 138; Antoninus Pius reigned from 138 to 161; and finally, Marcus Aurelius governed from 161 to 180. This was the Antonine Dynasty.

Trajan was the one who fought the most battles. They were violent campaigns that expanded the Empire to the north - beyond the Danube River into what is now Romania - and to the east, into Mesopotamia (Iraq). Emperor Hadrian, on the other hand, fought a second Jewish rebellion, which turned Jerusalem into a military colony. Aurelius, in turn, spent many years protecting the Danube region against invasion attempts.

These five emperors succeeded each other without records of assassinations or conspiracies. The first four ones, not having children of their own, followed the Roman tradition of adopting adults in order to find the best possible successor. Economically, everything was fine: taxes generated substantial revenue and foreign trade reached its peak. Additionally, the army remained obedient to the emperor's command.

This was the longest period in Roman history without a civil war since the 2nd century BCE. Most provinces were peaceful during this time. Hence, garrison troops were no longer necessary. Even Gaul, which had resisted Roman control in Julius Caesar's time, came under the control of a few men. The primary concern now was the maintenance of security on the borders.

6

CRUELTY AND INSANITY ON THE THRONE

ROMAN EMPERORS WERE TEMPERAMENTAL, ECCENTRIC, CAPRICIOUS AND SOME OF THEM SHOWED ATROCIOUS BEHAVIOR AGAINST THEIR OWN RELATIVES AND ADVERSARIES

Responsible for introducing the imperial period in Rome, Caesar Augustus was the first in the line of shrewd leaders who ruled with an iron fist. He brought stability to the Roman political environment, but indirectly, he also paved the way for cruel emperors with unorthodox behaviors.

The truth is that those in power exhibited a wide range of behaviors. Some accounts - not all confirmed by historians - suggest that even a horse was appointed to an important public position. Emperors were also known for their cruelty and greed, which reportedly led some to kill their own family members.

However, certain actions - such as the practice of incest - need to be regarded as relative, since they occurred nearly 2,000 years ago and in very different circumstances from today. In the following pages, the reader can delve into the profiles and behaviors of some of these men in more detail.

CAESAR AUGUSTUS, THE FIRST
EMPEROR BETWEEN 27 BCE AND 14 CE

In addition to being the first Roman emperor, there is no doubt that Gaius Julius Caesar Octavian Augustus was also one of the most important ones. He was born in the city of Rome - the capital of the Empire - in September 63 BCE and he died in August 14 CE in the Italian municipality of Nola. Augustus, who belonged to the Julio-Claudian Dynasty, had two children, Tiberius and Julia. He held Roman power for 41 years, from January 16th, 27 BCE, until his death.

During his government, Octavian organized military expeditions in regions including Raetia, Pannonia, Hispania, Germania, Arabia and Africa. He also pacified the Alpine regions and Hispania. Moreover, he annexed Galatia and Judea to the Empire. Many historians consider the Augustan period as one of the most prosperous in the Empire, both economically and culturally.

He was known as a moderate and energetic ruler. Implicitly, he wanted to leave the image of a great father who selflessly restored peace and prosperity to a people devastated by war. There is no doubt that Augustus was a generous patron to the poor, forcing the wealthy to make financial contributions to pay for the standing army and public works. However, beneath his benevolence there was a streak of cruelty. Many people, including friends and relatives, were killed in the proscriptions of 43 BCE. Many other citizens lost their homes in the confiscations that provided land for army veterans.

APPEARANCE

A century later, Suetonius, the biographer of Augustus, used many expressions to exalt the favorable image of the first Roman emperor. He emphasized that Octavian was "unusually handsome and extremely graceful at all periods of his life, although he did not care for personal adornment". The emperor also had bright, light colored eyes.

On the other hand, the biographer reports that Augustus had spaced, small and poorly kept teeth. His hair was slightly curly and apparently blond. His eyebrows joined together. On the other hand, his official images were carefully controlled and idealized. At the age of 19, his face first appeared on coins, a way to emphasize the image of the emperor.

TIBERIUS: EFFICIENT AND VICIOUS
EMPEROR BETWEEN 14 AND 37 CE

Tiberius Claudius Nero Caesar was born in 42 BCE and died in 37 CE He became the Roman emperor at the age of 56. He reigned from the death of his stepfather, Augustus, in 14 CE, until his own death.

He was the son of a previous marriage of Livia, Augustus's third wife. He was adopted and carried out diplomatic and military missions at the behest of the then-emperor. Victorious campaigns in Pannonia and Germany qualified him to be the successor in the Empire.

Tiberius was not the first choice of his stepfather. Nonetheless, Augustus had no other option since all his successive heirs had died, namely, Agrippa, Marcellus, Lucius and Gaius.

At the ceremony where he announced Tiberius as the heir to the throne, Caesar showed reluctance. So much so that, at the end of the speech, he said, "I do this for the sake of the State". History does not explain why he

Marble statue depicts Tiberius: cruelty marked the reign of the emperor

disliked his stepson, but many believe it was because Tiberius did not act as a bootlicker and often confronted him.

Tiberius spent a significant part of his reign on military campaigns, many of which secured the expansion of the empire's borders. In one of these battles, he lost his brother, Drusus, his companion in these endeavors.

The episode of the death of his Germanic nephew, in the East, marked the beginning of a government period characterized by violence and tyranny. In a highly deranged state, Tiberius killed his own wife, Julia, and the chief of the Praetorian Guard, Lucius Aelius Sejanus. He also ruthlessly executed family members, accomplices and friends.

In this period, important members of the Roman society were persecuted, tortured and killed, especially in the capital of the Empire. His reign is also marked by the crucifixion of Jesus Christ. His government helped promote the idea of the cult of the emperor and elevated the materialistic character of Rome. Positive aspects included improvements in public services, financial stability and discipline control in the army.

In 26 CE, Tiberius seemed weary of the political intrigues in the court. He left the capital and settled in Campania. In the following year, he went to the island of Capri, where he spent time with Greek intellectuals. He reportedly died naturally in 37 CE, although many believe he was assassinated in his own bed, under the orders of Caligula, by members of the Praetorian Guard.

CALIGULA AND MORAL DEBAUCHERY
EMPEROR BETWEEN 37 AND 41 CE

Gaius Caligula's father was a German, brave consul and general of the Roman Empire who died at just 34 years old, probably poisoned. Orphan in infancy, Caligula was adopted by Emperor Tiberius and was 25 years old when he succeeded his adoptive father and was named emperor. Over the years, he obtained all the imperial titles, including that of Augustus Caesar, which guaranteed him sovereign power over the entire nation.

He lived from the age of two in his father's military camp. He was very loved by the soldiers, who watched him grow. They were the ones who gave him the nickname with which he became famous. Caligula is the diminutive word for caliga, the military footwear worn by the Romans.

According to the historian Suetonius, Caligula participated in the murder of his adoptive father. Tiberius – who designated him as one of his heirs – was well aware of his distorted character and stated that he was preparing a viper for the Roman people. According to Tiberius himself, Caligula had all the vices of his parents and none of the virtues.

The liberal beginning of his government seemed to bode well for the population. However, the emperor fell ill due to excesses and orgies. When he was finally recovered, he showed his evil side. Some historians believe that the disease caused him to become demented. At that moment, he began to spend exorbitantly and to impose very high taxes. The final part of Caligula's reign was eventful.

He was known for complete debauchery in his sexual life. He was accused of having sex with his three sisters. However, his favorite diversion was torturing convicts in front of their families. He took the victims' possessions and he did not accept, in any way, being contradicted. He was also accused of ordering criminals to be served alive as a meal to wild animals.

He maintained a prostitution house and even gave orders for statues to be placed in prominent locations in all temples, including the synagogues in Jerusalem. It generated conflict with the Jews, who did not accept the emperor's desire at all. Caligula wanted to be worshiped as a true god.

Although the soldiers supported their leader's madness, the guard officers grew tired of so much insanity and decided to put an end to his mad government. In a conspiracy that brought together the guard and senators, the emperor was murdered in a tunnel that connected the Palace to the Forum.

CLAUDIUS: ADVANCES AND POLEMICS
EMPEROR BETWEEN 41 AND 54 CE

Appointed emperor by the Praetorians, Tiberius Claudius Caesar Augustus Germanicus was born in Lyon (10 BCE) and died in Rome (54 CE). Son of Nero Claudius Drusus and Antonia, he was the younger brother of Germanicus, the natural successor to the throne. Nevertheless, Germanicus died under rather strange circumstances: returning from Antioch, he was reportedly afflicted by an illness that proved fatal. The governor of Syria, Calpurnius Piso, disliked him and was accused of poisoning him or cursing him. With the support of the Praetorian Guard – which was fighting against the Senate's proposed restoration of the Republic – Claudius was placed as the great leader of the Roman government.

The emperor was lame and stuttered. As a child, he suffered from various diseases. They left his body weakened and his mind affected by a slight delay. He was considered a fool by his own mother. On the other hand, Claudius admitted to pretending to be slow-witted to go unnoticed by his nephew, Caligula, thus surviving the reign of horror.

Claudius was very dedicated to literature in his government. He began an unfinished work on Roman history. He also wrote more than two dozen books on the Etruscans and Carthaginians, an autobiography and a spelling reform project.

As a conqueror, in 42 CE, he annexed Mauritania in North Africa and in 53 CE, the island of Britain. He integrated Lycia, Judea and Thrace into the Empire and promoted the Romanization of the new provinces.

As a direct benefit to the people, he conducted important public works such as the construction of new aqueducts – which solved the problem of water supply in Rome –, the improvement of roads and the construction of a port in Ostia. Claudius' favorite pastime was watching criminals being tortured to death. He also ordered the execution of his third wife, Messalina, and 300 friends – including the famous actor Mnester. The truth is that he suspected his wife of promoting orgies with these men.

In the end, he was assassinated by his fourth wife, Agrippina II, after adopting her son, Nero, as his successor. Claudius was poisoned with mushrooms. It was with Caesar that the famous phrase of the gladiators originated: "Hail Caesar! We who are about to die salute you".

NERO AND HIS SHAMEFUL GOVERNMENT
EMPEROR BETWEEN 54 AND 68 CE

Born in Antium on December 15, 37 CE, Tiberius Nero Claudius Domitian Caesar became the ruler of Rome at the age of 17. His ascent to power was the result of a plot planned by his mother, Agrippina, and the philosopher Seneca, his mentor. They convinced Claudius to adopt him shortly before his death.

However, as soon as he assumed the position, Nero came into conflict with his mother, who aspired to rule Rome through her son. Over time, she began to consider the possibility of changing the throne occupant. Seneca, however, arranged the death of one of the contenders.

Seneca himself and the prefect of Rome, Sextus Afranius, were Nero's advisors. The first five years of his reign, in fact, were considered one of the happiest periods of the Empire. His mentors allowed him to indulge in all of his passions. In return, he had to allow himself to be guided by them in his government.

Meanwhile, Nero's mother, Agrippina, sought to regain the lost authority over her son. Nevertheless, in 59 CE, the emperor had her killed. Some say she was his only moral restraint. After her murder, Nero became a tyrannical leader, and over time, he became known as one of Rome's most shameful emperors. He then married Poppaea Sabina after divorcing

FOLKLORIC DECISIONS

Claudius was not only efficient in government and vicious in dealing with his enemies. He also took bizarre measures. The main one was the liberation of free flatulence during the banquets!

Octavia, who was also subsequently killed at his command.

Around the same time, Sextus Afranius died and Nero appointed Otho, a ruthless individual, as his advisor. The emperor's decision led Seneca to resign from his position.

This period was marked by Nero's obsession with being admired. Nero's passionate love for the dramatic arts and spectacles led him to act as a poet and musician. His desire to be famous for various accomplishments also drove him to participate in chariot races, perhaps the Empire's main entertainment.

The fire that destroyed part of Rome in 64 CE was not ordered by him, despite many accusations. So, Nero decided to blame the Christians, who were already hated and began to be persecuted. According to tradition, he had the apostle Peter crucified and Paul of Tarsus beheaded. In 65 CE, Nero, at the height of his madness, killed Poppaea – who was pregnant – with a kick to the abdomen.

Extreme cruelty and the waste of public resources led to growing opposition against him. Such conspiracies were suppressed three times, and those involved were forced to commit suicide. He became paranoid. The fear of being killed haunted him. Therefore, he established a regime of terror and tried to maintain popularity by donating huge amounts of wheat.

In the year 66 CE, he married Messalina and embarked on a two-year tour of the Greek islands, a long-standing desire. At the end of the trip, Nero liberated Greece from Roman rule and made it an independent State.

However, upon returning to the capital of the Empire, he was faced with a chaotic situation. Rebellions were taking place at that time in the most important provinces of Rome, such as Gaul, Germania, Africa, Lusitania, Syria and Egypt. Nero was also betrayed by Otho and no longer had the support of the Praetorian Guard. Regarded as the Senate's main enemy, Nero's only alternative was to flee and kill himself. His suicide at the age of 30 ended the Julio-Claudian Dynasty.

VESPASIAN, THE NORMAL
EMPEROR BETWEEN 69 AND 79 CE

Titus Flavius Sabinus Vespasian was born in the year 9, in the Sabine region near Rieti, and died in 79 CE. He ended up being proclaimed emperor by the soldiers in Alexandria. As the first upper-class commoner to rise to such a high and prestigious office, he initiated the Flavian Dynasty.

The philosopher Seneca was Nero's great tutor

Coin containing Vespasian's face, responsible for instauring order in Rome

RESURRECTED?

Even after his death, Nero continued to be highly regarded by poor Romans. So much so that, for three times, many of them believed that he had reappeared in the East, which helped to fuel the myth of "Nero redivivus".

Historians assert that he was very humble and hardworking. He brought order to the military, pacified the provinces, and continued the process of conquering Britain. He also fought the Jewish rebellion in 66 CE and brutally defeated them in 70 CE, when Jerusalem was destroyed by the hands of his son, Colonel Titus.

He was also quite effective in economic administration, both in the capital and the provinces. It was enabled primarily by an increase in annual taxes and a significant reduction in public expenditures. The Empire's sound financial health even facilitated fund-raising for the construction of the Temple of Peace - dedicated to Jupiter Capitolinus - and also for the Colosseum in Rome. He died of natural causes.

BRIEF REIGN OF TITUS
EMPEROR BETWEEN 79 AND 81 CE

Titus Flavius Vespasianus Augustus was born on December 30th, 39 CE, in Rome. He was the eldest son and successor of Vespasian. He left the throne due to his death on September 13th, 81 CE. He is best remembered as the general who, during Vespasian's reign, defeated the rebellion in the province of Judea (in the year 66 CE) and destroyed Jerusalem (in 70 A.D).

During his reign, the famous eruption of Mount Vesuvius occurred, engulfing Pompeii, Herculaneum and Stabiae in August of 79 CE. In Pompeii alone, 16 thousand people perished, approximately 80% of the city's population.

Despite this tragedy, his popularity did not wane. Even to this day, works in his honor in the historic center of Rome can be seen. The most famous one is the Arch of Titus, a 50-foot-high marble monument that celebrates his victory in Judea. Carved on the arch are depictions of the table of showbread, silver trumpets, and the seven-branched menorah, symbols of Judaism.

THE TYRANNY OF DOMITIAN
EMPEROR BETWEEN 81 AND 96 CE

TTitus Flavius Domitianus, born on October 24th, 51 CE, became emperor after the death of his older brother, Titus, in 81 CE. Some say that he was responsible for his brother's death and that he coldly executed a cousin during his rule.

Nonetheless, his abuses began when his father Vespasian was still emperor. Domitian forced Domitia Longina, Elius Lamia's legitimate wife, to divorce him and marry Domitian instead. As emperor, he limited the powers of the senators, taking on the responsibility to appoint governors for the provinces, and he also established the Council of Princes, which superseded the Senate. Furthermore, he accumulated the titles of consul and perpetual censor. In addition, he was heavily involved in the reconstruction of monuments, where he usually had his name engraved without even mentioning the founder's name. He even prohibited statues of himself on the Capitoline Hill unless they were made of gold or silver.

With a reprehensible character, Domitian faced increasing pressure and sought to secure his grip on power by becoming bloodthirsty and cruel. His opponents were tortured and summarily executed. Over the years, he also began to demand to be treated as a god. During this time, he initiated the second persecution of Christians.

Faced with such tyranny, he was killed in a conspiracy on September 18th, 96 CE. Some of his friends and even his wife, Domitia Longina, were believed to have participated in the uprising against him. After his assassination, the Senate, horrified by this malevolent figure, declared him damned and erased his name from Roman monuments.

TRAJAN: INBORN ADMINISTRATOR
EMPEROR BETWEEN 98 AND 117 CE

Emperor Trajan, whose full name was Marcus Ulpius Nerva Trajanus,

TRAJAN'S COLUMN

In his expansionist campaigns, Trajan advanced on the Dacians, who lived in a land rich in gold and silver – where Romania and Hungary are currently located.

The territorial conquest occurred after two major wars between the years 101 and 105. The military campaign is documented in the monument called Trajan's Column, which can still be found in the center of Rome today.

The stone column, erected in 113, in front of the Forum of Rome, is full of images of the battle in bas-relief that spiral up throughout the monument. The column is 98 feet high and more than 11 feet in diameter.

was born on September 18th, 53 CE, in Hispania. He came from a noble family and received military training. At the age of 38, he was appointed consul and was adopted by Emperor Nerva as his successor. The victories achieved in military campaigns were the reason why he earned so much prestige.

When Nerva passed away, Trajan received support from the Senate and, over time, proved to be an excellent administrator. He reorganized the Empire, revitalizing agriculture and trade. Despite reducing the tax burden, he sponsored significant projects for the Romans. He also led territorial conquests that brought Rome to its greatest territorial extent in history.

The final part of his reign was marked by wars. Ironically, while returning from a battle near the Black Sea, Trajan died, probably due to a heart attack, on August 8th, 117 CE.

HADRIAN, ART LOVER
EMPEROR BETWEEN 117 AND 138 CE

Born in the year 76 in Italica (modern-day Spain), Hadrian ruled from 117 to 138 CE. He was Trajan's nephew, who was also his great mentor. Hadrian was known as a highly skilled administrator, as well as a tireless traveler. He traveled throughout the Roman Empire to assess the situation of the provinces and ensure the necessary adjustments and reforms.

He also implemented a profound reform in administration and, in the year 131, he issued a code of laws to be used throughout the Empire, the

Trajan became known for his military and administrative competency

Hadrian was emperor and a poet

Perpetual Edict. It was a legal compilation that governed Rome until the time of Justinian.

Hadrian abandoned Trajan's campaigns in Mesopotamia and adopted a defensive policy, fortifying the borders of the Roman Empire. In England, he ordered the construction of Hadrian's Wall in 112, which marked the border between England and Scotland for centuries to defend it from northern peoples.

However, the government was not his greatest passion. He was more interested in literature and arts in general. On his deathbed, he composed the poem Animula, which means little soul:

"*Little soul, roamer and charmer,*
My body's comrade and its sometime guest,
What dominion now must be your goal,
Pale and stiff and naked?
Unable now, like us, to jest."

Hadrian also drew inspiration from Greek culture to make Rome more beautiful. The empire was filled with monuments: he had the Hadrian's Villa built, as well as the Sant'Angelo Bridge and the Castle of the same name, his mausoleum.

ANTONINUS PIUS, THE PEACEFUL
EMPEROR BETWEEN 138 AND 161 CE

Antoninus became known as a man detached from power

PRESUMPTION OF INNOCENCE PRINCIPLE

Very just, Antoninus Pius brought together, during his mandate, a team of legal experts who helped him in the work of revising the Roman legislation. Even today he is credited with the principle that every man must be considered innocent until proven guilty.

Roman Emperor from 138 to 161, Antoninus Pius contrasts with many of the bitter figures who ruled the Empire. He was born in Lanuvium in 86 CE and came from the traditional bourgeoisie of Latium. He was a man who held respect for both people and deities. He was even called the perfect Emperor due to his gentleness, serene demeanor and lack of attachment to glory. Moreover, he willingly accepted advice from friends.

Unlike most Roman emperors, Antoninus greatly loved his wife. One of the best-preserved monuments in the Roman Forum is the Temple of Antoninus and Faustina, which was built in 141 CE in honor of his wife. The site was later dedicated to the emperor upon his death in 161 CE.

THE PHILOSOPHER MARCUS AURELIUS
EMPEROR BETWEEN 121 AND 180 CE

Born on April 26, 121 A.D., in Rome, Marcus Aurelius Antoninus came from an aristocratic family but lost his parents at a young age. He was adopted by his uncle Aurelius Antoninus - who also later became emperor. Shortly thereafter, he was named as his successor.

At the age of 11, he was introduced to the ideas of Stoicism – a doctrine that emphasizes the eradication of passions and the resigned acceptance of fate as characteristics of a wise man. He dedicated himself to the study of philosophy and some rhetoric. Formally educated, he held the position of consul three times. After Antoninus's death, he became co-emperor alongside Lucius Verus. When Verus died in 169, Marcus Aurelius became the sole ruler of the throne.

The reign of Marcus Aurelius was marked by prolonged wars and by a series of internal challenges. He was an excellent warrior and administrator and yet he humanized the exercise of power to an extreme degree.

Whenever possible, he engaged in philosophical reflection and wrote his thoughts in the Greek language. He thus became the third and last exponent of Roman Stoicism. The content of his "Meditations" is imbued with this philosophy, albeit a Stoicism distant from the doctrines of Zeno, founder of this school of thought. Physical and logical speculations gave way to the practical character of the Romans and moral guidance.

THE INSANITIES OF COMMODUS
EMPEROR BETWEEN 177 AND 192 CE

Commodus can be described as a spoiled boy. Son of Marcus Aurelius and Faustina, he was born on August 31st, 161. He was made Caesar by his father at the tender age of 5, and by the age of 16, he became Augustus. He participated in the Danube Wars alongside his father for two years. He became the sole emperor upon the death of Marcus Aurelius in 180.

In reality Commodus had very little interest in matters related to the government or the Empire. His life was an eternal feast, with a harem of 300 women and 300 men. Despite his lack of commitment, he was sensible enough to appoint capable individuals for the administration of the provinces.

He was a rather peculiar individual. Unlike his father, he greatly enjoyed combat and even participated in gladiatorial contests. However, unlike typical contests, the emperor was never in danger: his opponents always let him win and had their lives spared. As if it were not enough, Commodus believed himself to be the demigod Hercules and demanded that everyone worship him.

Commoduss led a fully unruly life

He ordered the assassination of his sister Lucilla and senators who conspired against him. However, his reign of excess came to an end when he was strangled by one of his allies during a bath. Under the rule of Septimius Severus, Commodus was posthumously deified.

CARACALLA: ANOTHER INSANE MAN IN POWER
EMPEROR BETWEEN 211 AND 217 CE

He was born on April 4th, 188, in what is now Lyon, France. He was the son of Emperor Septimius Severus and Julia Domna. He ruled Rome for six years. His administrative achievements are much less known than his insane actions.

Shortly after his adolescence, his psychological instability caused great concern to those around him. It is said that one day he tried to stab his own father in the back in front of the entire Roman army. He also despised his wife and sentenced her to exile before having her killed.

HELIOGABALUS
EMPEROR BETWEEN 218 AND 222 CE

Heliogabalus was another emperor known for his extremely eccentric behavior. As an example, he publicly castrated himself in the name of a religious cult. In another episode, he attempted to force the Romans to worship a foreign god.

ALEXANDER, THE GREAT

The emperor Caracalla was considered a fanatical admirer of Alexander, The Great. Therefore, without ceremony, he began to use the same garments and to behave like him.

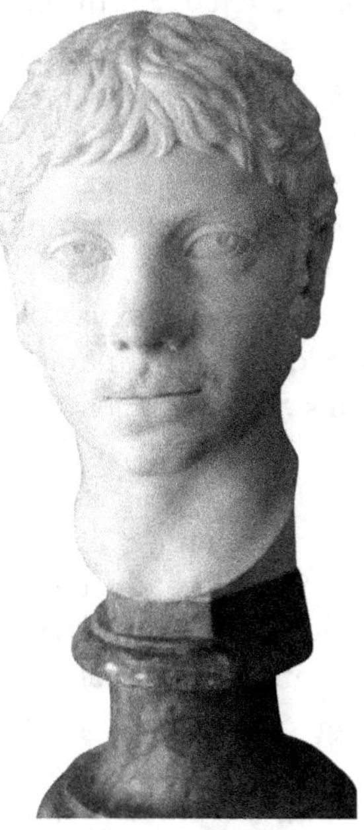

Emperor Heliogabalus castrated himself due to a religious cult

7

BREAD AND CIRCUSES: SOLUTION TO AN UNEQUAL EMPIRE

NOT EVEN THE IMPOSINGNESS OF ITS BUILDINGS AND MILITARY VICTORIES COULD HIDE THE SOCIAL DIFFERENCES PREVAILING IN ANCIENT ROME; IMPLEMENTATION OF POPULIST POLITICS WAS A WAY TO WHITEWASH THE PROBLEMS

The capital of the Roman Empire, founded in the 8th century BCE, is considered one of the pioneering cities in the Western world when it comes to organization. This society was based on the civilization of Ancient Greece. Hence, Rome managed to strengthen its customs, refine its political and religious systems and also structure trade and residential areas as a whole. It was an excellent example of efficient governance, as it was the center of this vast empire - which extended from the Iberian Peninsula to Egypt and Syria.

However, alongside wealth, the conquests also brought about social problems, particularly from the 2nd century BCE onwards. During its peak, the city of Rome approached the mark of two million inhabitants. This vast population was composed of men and women from very different social classes. There were several peasants who lost their jobs on the farms due to slavery, as well as street artists, artisans, members of the common people, members of the nobility and even politicians.

Therefore, the differences could be easily observed even by the most ignorant newcomer. Those who comprised the elite owned grand residences and opulent palaces. Meanwhile, the vast majority of the population squeezed into multi-story buildings with small apartments lacking kitchens and bathrooms. It seemed like only a matter of time before more significant urban problems began to emerge.

Picture showing street artists performing in the streets in Ancient Rome

WHERE PROBLEMS AROSE

The territorial expansion of the Empire, still in the Republican era, was crucial for profound social transformations in Rome. Right from the start, the economy, which had an agropastoral aspect, began to compete with a well-organized trade system between various regions located around the Mediterranean.

The increase in the number of slaves available for labor also led to a rise in the food supply. Meanwhile, magistrates and generals benefited from the administration and collection of taxes in the provinces of the new power. Simultaneously, the control of the patricians over the Senate made this class even wealthier through the expansion of their properties and the extensive use of slave labor.

On the one hand, there was incredible and growing wealth production; on the other hand, this new scenario brought immense losses to small landowners, as they could no longer compete equally with the prices of food offered by shrewd patricians. Furthermore, plebeians lost work opportunities due to the use of slaves in agriculture and animal husbandry.

As for the other plebeians who were part of the long ranks of the Roman army, they began to benefit from the conquest of land and servants. These members of the plebeian class, known as knights, earned considerable sums of money through tax collection, distribution of food to the armies, leasing of forested areas and mines, as well as the construction of bridges and roads. Their full control over these activities was reinforced

Present-day landscape of Rome: buildings where poor people lived were precarious

when senators and their descendants were eventually prohibited from engaging in any activity other than agriculture.

Those plebeians who could not amass wealth were compelled to sell their land to some big landowner. With no other alternative, they moved to the city. Upon arrival, they faced another significant problem: the lack of job opportunities. The easy access to slave labor narrowed employment prospects.

SEWER AND HEALTH

Numerous infrastructure projects in Ancient Rome were impressive for their time. Architecture and engineering were extensively used in the region to provide quality public services to the capital. Aqueducts known for their ingenuity, stadiums - like the famous Colosseum - and special gardens were some of the specialties of the Roman people.

The major issue, however, was that the vast majority of these interventions only benefited the wealthier. A clear example of this was the sewer systems – designed to ensure the proper disposal of waste from homes – constructed exclusively in the noblest areas of the city.

This situation posed an additional difficulty: without a proper system, the rest of the Roman population was simply forced to throw excrement out of their apartment windows. Some individuals carried buckets down to the street to have them emptied by people who made a living by collecting human waste to sell to farmers, who used it as fertilizer. The unpleasant odor in the streets was not the only source of extreme discomfort, as this practice also significantly increased the risk of serious diseases spreading through contamination.

Public officials attempted to ensure that these wastes were disposed of outside the residential areas of the city, but they were too limited a number to enforce this rule effectively. During the rule of Augustus (27 BCE – 14 CE), the residents of Rome generated approximately 132 thousand pounds of human waste per day. Archaeological excavations revealed the existence of hundreds of deep pits filled with a decomposing mixture of corpses, animal carcasses and all kinds of sewage not far from the city center on Esquiline Hill. This area was demarcated with signs that read: "Gaius Sentius, son of Gaius, as the praetor and by order of the Senate, established this boundary line of stones to mark the area that must be kept free of filth, animal carcasses, and corpses. It is also strictly prohibited to burn corpses here".

As the sanitary problem worsened, more people fell ill. The inability to keep the city clean meant that flies were present almost everywhere, and people suffered frequent intestinal issues caused by contaminated food and water. Moreover, there was no adequate medical treatment. Since only the wealthiest had some access to medical care, so many ordinary people suffered without any hope of being cured.

It is worth noting that even the nobles were at risk as medicine was still in its infancy. Roman treatments generally relied on medicinal herbs, whose knowledge was passed down from parents to children as a tradition, inherited through generations. Homemade remedies often included a touch of superstition. Mystical and often extravagant formulas were imposed on the sick. For instance, they believed in the possibility of expelling the illness. As an example, the wealthiest individuals of the time wore a popular jewel that, according to belief, prevented stomachaches.

AGGLOMERATES

The infrastructure in the city of Rome did not grow at the same rate as the urban population. An increasing number of buildings were constructed to accommodate the influx of people settling in the capital. However, this measure was far from sufficient to alleviate the main difficulties. The streets were becoming overcrowded. The roads served as workplaces for various professionals: merchants and laborers crowded into suffocating spaces. Numerous street vendors used thoroughfares as their only display counters. Others who competed for public spaces were street mountebanks (actors who performed on the streets) and animal trainers. Carriages and sedan chairs - used to transport the wealthy - shared the space with all these people, and traffic was too intense.

Furthermore, the city's buildings were at serious risk of collapsing. Despite their knowledge of stone, concrete and brick usage, Roman engineers lacked the technology to precisely calculate how much stress the structures could bear. Another problem was that construction workers tried, in every possible way, to reduce costs without considering engineering protection measures. This led Emperor Caesar Augustus to limit the height of apartment buildings to 68 feet.

The buildings of the poorer residents were also susceptible to flooding, as they were located in low-lying areas. The sunny hills sheltered the luxurious homes of the rich.

The chaotic situation generated significant discomfort among the common people. Faced with the alarming urban landscape, the plebeians began to think that they could make strong demands to obtain better living conditions and more dignified lifestyles. Therefore, they initiated some uprisings. However, these demonstrations were met with violence by the Roman army and quickly suppressed.

Around the 1st century BCE, the large number of slaves also transformed this subordinate class into a powerful and threatening political force in the Roman world. In 71 BCE, the gladiator Spartacus organized a revolt that brought together tens of thousands of slaves against Roman army troops. Thanks to the actions of Roman generals, the uprising was contained. Nevertheless, it served as a warning of the growing tensions within the territory that could even lead to a civil war. It was high time for the government to take action to prevent the complete loss of control over the internal situation. That was a matter of what plan would be executed by the leaders

BREAD AND CIRCUSES

In order to calm the mood, the Roman Empire sought to adopt a measure that would ensure at least adequate food for the neediest population. The policy of Bread and Circuses (panem et circenses) was established by Caesar Augustus. The phrase, in fact, originates from Satire X, by the Roman poet and humorist Juvenal, who lived around the year 100 CE. In its original context, the artist criticized the lack of information among the people, who, according to him, had no interest in political matters and only wanted food and entertainment.

In this time, the Colosseum and other grand stadiums were built for events such as gladiator fights – which became major spectacles – and chariot racing, for example. During these events, the population attended for entertainment, but they also received food and wheat abundantly. Additionally, another imperial tradition was the monthly distribution of cereals in the Portico of Minucius.

In general, these "indulgences" for the people ensured that the plebeians would not starve or become bored. The advantage of this practice was that, at the same time, the population was content and pacified and the emperor's popularity among the most humble was solidified. It was the best and most immediate way to keep the people under government control.

FOOD

It's important to highlight that the distribution of grains at cost price or even for free was a decades-old tradition, from long before the adoption of this more populist policy. Throughout most of the Republic era, the supply of cereals was part of the duties of the so-called aediles. This supply was personified as a goddess, and the grain quota was ultimately distributed from the temple of Ceres. In 440 BCE, the Roman Senate appointed an official for this role: the prefect of provisions. The holder of this office had significant powers. The emergency grain supply was an important source of influence and power for the consul Pompey the Great (106 BCE - 48 BCE) later in his career. During the principate period, the position of prefect of provisions became permanent and a range of privileges, including citizenship grants and exemption from duties, were offered to ship captains who signed contracts to transport grains to the city.

Nonetheless, Augustus increased the number of citizens assisted by using his personal fortune to buy imported grains. It is estimated that the first Roman emperor provided for around 250 thousand men. Since many of them had families, statistics suggest that up to 700 thousand people depended on his regime for basic food.

The poor would turn the grain - which was not the most suitable for baking bread - into a watery porridge, served with cheap wine. If they were lucky, they might have beans, leeks and even some pieces of meat. Meanwhile, the rich indulged in more delightful dishes like roast pork or lobster.

Most of the supply was obtained through the free market. This was because prices in Rome were very high, as traders sought excessive profits. Interestingly, cereals were also collected as tribute in certain provinces by soldiers and officials, who then resold them.

Over time, the supply gained a higher status. During the reign of Septimius Severus (193 - 211), olive oil was added to the ration. However, during the rule of Aurelian (270 - 275), a major reorganization of the provision was performed. He is said to have ceased the distribution of cereals. Instead, he began to give or sell bread, salt, pork and wine at a low price. These measures continued with his successors.

With the devaluation of the currency in the 3rd century, the Roman army began to be paid with supplies and also in cash through a heavy system of supply collection and redistribution. The State's role in providing cereals continued to be a central point of its unity and power.

ENTERTAINMENT

Roman pastimes were not very diverse. They were primarily focused on chariot races, theatrical performances, gladiator contests, spectacles with wild animals and naval battles. These public entertainments were encouraged and funded by the government or by patricians.

The venues for these events were stadiums or amphitheaters, oval or circular buildings with bleachers and an arena in the middle where presentations, combats and other games took place. On spectacle days, musicians would play. The most common instruments included lyres, flutes, cymbals, bagpipes, trumpets and rattles

GLADIATORS

Gladiator fights became one of the main entertainments in Rome. However, few people are familiar with the reality of these fighters. Gladiators were typically slaves in Ancient Rome. The term used to refer to these men, forced to fight, comes from gladius, the name of a short double-edged sword they wielded.

According to historians, the earliest records of gladiator fights in Roman territory date back to 286 BCE. Nevertheless, it is known that this was a "sport" invented by the Etruscans. Thus, it quickly gained popularity among the residents of Rome. Its success was immediate and attracted an increasingly larger audience.

Originally, the combatants would fight in the arena, and a winner was only declared when one of them died, lost their weapons or was unable to continue fighting. There was always a supervisor - a kind of referee - who determined whether the defeated man should be killed or spared. In these cases, the people in the stands strongly influenced the decision. Typically, spectators would signal their desire by either giving a thumbs-down gesture, indicating they wanted the defeated man to be killed, or a thumbs-up gesture, indicating they wanted the defeated man's life to be spared at that moment.

For several centuries, gladiators not only fought each other but also against fierce animals, brought from the African territories. In addition to slaves, prisoners of war and criminals of more serious crimes were frequent participants in these bloody battles.

In order to fight, gladiators underwent rigorous training in specialized arena combat schools. They also received special treatment during breaks between bouts and typically did not fight more than three times a year. Hence, being a gladiator was much more advantageous than being a common Roman slave and it also offered a unique opportunity for general public recognition.

When traveling to fight in other cities, gladiators moved in groups known as families and were often escorted by trainers. In contrast to what many might imagine, gladiators were generally vegetarians.

To ensure balanced battles, fighters were divided into categories, including: Thracians, murmillos, retiarii, secutores and dimachaeri. Studies conducted on the skeletons of these combatants have shown that those judged by the audience and sentenced to death were often killed through a fatal strike to the jugular. When a fighter was too weakened, they would get down on all fours and get a strong blow to the back, which hit the heart directly.

These spectacles were held on approximately 182 days of the year. After many centuries of gladiator fights, the practice was officially banned by Emperor Constantine I, in 325, with the rise of Christianity. The battles continued clandestinely for another century, but it was Pope Innocent I and Emperor Honorius who managed to decree the definitive end of this practice.

COLOSSEUM

Certain constructions are true symbols of specific locations and their culture. So was the Colosseum, synonymous with fights between gladiators. Majestic, it was more comfortable than many modern soccer stadiums.

The construction began in 72 CE, by order of Emperor Flavius Vespasian, who decided to build the arena on the location of a former palace of Nero, his predecessor on the Roman throne. The grand work took eight years to be completed, and when it was fully ready, Rome was already ruled by Vespasian's son, General Titus. To pay tribute to his father, he named the place "Vespasian Amphitheater". The seating capacity revolved around 50,000 people and the fighting area - the arena itself - measured 278 by 173 feet.

According to some historians, the name Colosseum was probably given a few hundred years later, perhaps in the 11th century. It may have been inspired by Nero's Colossus, a sumptuous bronze statue with an estimated height of 114 feet. The statue is located right next to the amphitheater.

The first fights held to celebrate the completion of the Colosseum are said to have lasted about 100 days. In this period alone, it is estimated that hundreds of gladiators and more than 5,000 wild and fierce animals would have been killed in the place. The games drove the ecstatic audience crazy. In addition to the grandstands, which were 9 feet above the ground, there was a cabin very close to the arena intended for the Emperor of Rome. From that spot, the fighters would make the greeting that would become internationally known through the centuries: "Hail, Caesar! We who are about to die salute you".

CHARIOT RACING

The chariot was a widely used combat vehicle in antiquity. Today, it is commonly represented in artistic depictions and movies that portray the period. The chariot was an important resource for battles. Essentially, it was a model of a war car propelled by two horses pulling a carriage, on which the combatants would move, supported by two wheels.

However, this mode of transportation and combat was not exclusive to the Romans. The chariot was used in various parts of the ancient world and gained success and recognition due to the invention of spokes in the wheel. The relief and weight distribution put less strain on the horses, which, in general, were too small to bear the weight of the combatants for long periods of time on the battlefield.

Therefore, the vehicle also came to be used to enhance the entertainment of the Bread and Circuses policy. With the Romans, this sport even had connotations of being the Formula 1 of Antiquity, with organized teams, sponsors and highly popular riders.

The teams were divided by colors. There were races with two horses (bigae) and races with four horses (quadrigae). The racers could be slaves or free men, but they made a lot of money and could become rich and famous. The problem was that the vehicles had little stability and a strong tendency to overturn in the curves. The teams belonged to private individuals and the prizes were high. The mad Emperor Nero participated in the races - and always won as he was the governor. Chariot races only ceased to exist in Rome with the collapse of the State.

It was one of the favorite pastimes of the population. It was a distraction that helped perpetuate the social differences among citizens, who were numbed by the entertainment provided by the Empire.

After the prohibition of gladiator fights in the 4th century, the Colosseum had various other uses. It was used, for example, as a setting for simulated naval battles, on occasions when the area of the arena was completely flooded. In the Middle Ages, the marble and bronze of the structure were gradually looted and used to adorn churches and other Catholic monuments. Marble pieces from the amphitheater were even used in the construction of the famous Saint Peter's Basilica in the Vatican. In the 11th century, the Colosseum was transformed into a fortress, sheltering members of a noble family, the Frangipane, who used the building to protect themselves in their battles against rival groups.

Current picture showing the internal area of the Colosseum, which held more than 50 thousand people in its golden times

Even in ruins today, the Colosseum still inspires a majesty that impresses tourists from around the world who visit the Italian capital. Located right in the center of the city, it receives more than 3 million visitors each year. Those who walk inside the building can at least feel a little bit of the atmosphere of the grand amphitheater.

END OF POPULIST MEASURES

Despite the success it achieved, the populist policy of "Bread and Circuses" could not survive indefinitely. The capital, Rome, experienced a process of decline due to popular dissatisfaction, invasions by other peoples and the spread of diseases and plagues. Along with the Empire itself, the mentioned practice also disappeared, which had worked quite effectively while the foundation of the Roman politics remained strong.

Some believe that even today, many governments employ similar measures to manipulate the masses. For them, the tactics adopted in Rome almost two thousand years ago still have relevance through sporting events and high-appeal television shows.

8

AN IMPERIAL ECONOMY

EVEN AMID WARS AND INTERNAL CONFLICTS, ANCIENT ROME REMAINED ECONOMICALLY VIGOROUS FOR A LONG TIME

The Roman economy was the foundation of the Empire's strength during its centuries of dominance. Reflecting all the wealth acquired, there were impressive constructions in the capital and a very powerful army feared by all the peoples in the ancient world. Despite the increasing social problems over the years, the financial power of the empire remained high and was only shaken with the decline of Rome from the 4th century onwards.

However, before the extensive territorial expansion, the economic sector was based on diverse agricultural activities. Agriculture and livestock played a fundamental role since 90% of the population lived in the countryside. The main products were typical of the Mediterranean culture: grains, olives, fruits, wine and livestock. The wealthiest individuals owned large agricultural estates, while vast latifundia were cultivated by slaves.

In this period of Roman history, there were no monetary transactions. Trade and craftsmanship, on the other hand, were still underdeveloped.

With the integration of vast territories into the Empire, there was a progressive growth in trade, favored by the Pax Romana (Roman Peace). Different Roman provinces had different resources, and they intensified trade between them, supported by an extensive network of roads, navigable rivers and the Mediterranean Sea, where maritime transportation was safer and cheaper.

Products from all over the Empire reached Rome. This growth in trade increased agricultural and artisanal production, as well as currency circulation. Cities in the Empire gained dynamism, especially in the privileged trade hubs, where small artisan workshops proliferated, attracting peasants to the cities in search of better living conditions. This marked a period of intense rural exodus.

Cities constituted the center of the political and administrative life of the Empire, where emperors and the wealthiest individuals chose to build public buildings - baths, theaters and amphitheaters - to attract inhabitants. By the 2nd century BCE, there were already about 4,000 cities throughout the Empire.

Specialization in manufacturing, agriculture and mining was a noticeable trend. Certain provinces were more focused on cultivating specific types of products, such as grains in Egypt and North Africa, and wine and olive oil in Italy, Hispania and Greece.

Nevertheless, knowledge of the Roman economy is considered irregular and inconsistent. The vast majority of traded products, primarily agricultural, typically do not leave direct archaeological evidence. Very rarely, as in Berenice, there is evidence of long-distance trade of items like pepper, almonds, hazelnuts, pine nuts, walnuts, coconuts, apricots and peaches, in addition to the more expected products like figs, raisins and capers. The sales of wine, olive oil and garum (fermented fish sauce) were specifically made in amphorae, which left archaeological records. On the other hand, there is a single reference in Syria concerning the export of marmalade to the capital, Rome.

What is certain is that exports grew, and the Romans embarked on a path of significant economic development. Faced with favorable conditions, urban centers expanded, as the construction of new roads and slave labor created an attractive environment.

TRADE

Commercial transactions in Rome were extremely important during most of the imperial era. Some may neglect this sector today, but there is no denying that trade not only helped expand the Latin lingua franca but also sustained the achievements of the legions. It is worth noting that the

AGRICULTURAL TECHNIQUES

Methods for achieving better efficiency in Roman agriculture – irrigation, drainage and also land recovery – guaranteed an adequate supply of food, leading to a rapid increase in urban populations.

In the dry lands of the Mediterranean, water reserves were created for irrigation through the construction of large and sophisticated dams.

On the other hand, in the lands to the east of Britain and on the Padan Plain, marshy lowlands were reclaimed through extensive drainage channels' nets. The use of water mills has also been known since Ancient Rome.

Romans were businessmen and the longevity of the Empire is largely attributed to commercial relationships.

Local society was segmented around commercial areas and activities. Members of the Senate and their children, for example, were restricted to commerce. Members of the equestrian order were known for diversifying their businesses, although those of higher status placed greater emphasis on military and leisure activities. Meanwhile, common citizens and freedpeople ran shops and stalls in markets. As for a countless number of slaves, they performed all sorts of heavy labor. These very slaves, in fact, were the subject of quite profitable commercial transactions.

UNITS OF MEASUREMENT

The inhabitants of Ancient Rome were known as sophisticated engineers. As a result, they had well-defined units of measurement for lengths, weights and distances. The Roman measurement system was built based on the Greek system, with some influences from Egypt. The Roman weight units were known for their precision. Distances were systematically measured and inscribed on stones by government agents.

For commercial trade, the amphora served as a convenient measure for liquids. It contained a Roman cubic foot, equivalent to about 1.8 gallons. The standard amphora - known as Capitoline Amphora - was kept in the Temple of Jupiter on the Capitoline Hill in Rome, so that others could compare their amphoras to it.

Although Egypt and some provinces issued their own coins, the Romans reasonably standardized the currency exchange rate around the 2nd century BCE, which greatly facilitated trade in the main city of the empire.

Roman coins, in circulation during most of the Roman Republic and the Western Roman Empire, included the aureus[1] (made of gold), the denarius (made of silver), the sestertius and the dupondius (both made of bronze), as well as the as (made of copper). These denominations were used until the mid-3rd century. After reforms, the coins in circulation mainly became the solidus (minted in gold) and some smaller bronze denominations, which persisted until the end of the Western Roman Empire.

---

[1]   Coin represented on the cover, equivalent to 25 silver denaruises. (Editor's note)

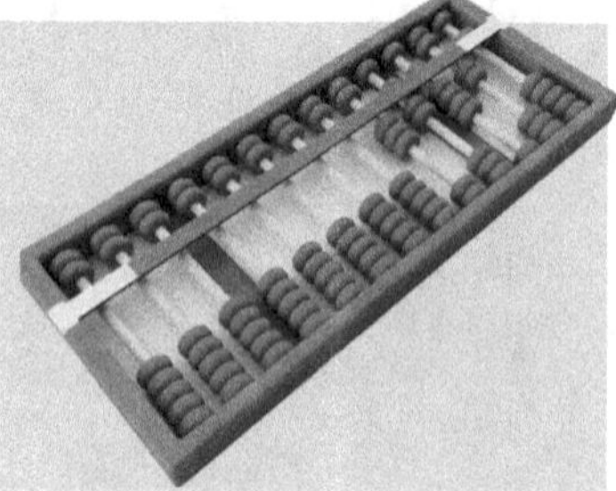

ROMAN CALCULATOR

The complicated accounting of Rome's trade was done, above all, by using tables and the abacus.

The second one, which used Roman numerals, was ideal for counting coins and recording weight measurements.

Image of denarius, one of the coins used in the Roman Empire

BARGAINING

Roman society was also characterized by the presence of individuals known as negotiators, mainly active during the later years of the Republic. They were citizens established in the provinces who lent money at interest. They also traded grains, speculating on and profiting from the fluctuations in the price of the primary food source of that time. They typically sent grains to Rome and beyond the borders.

However, their primary business was indeed money loans at interest. Therefore, the words negotiator, negociate and negotiation were used with that meaning during that period. According to the philosopher Cicero, they were simply "businessmen" and played a fundamental role in organizing markets, investing in transportation and providing credit, facilitating new enterprises. The term "negotiator" was held in higher esteem. Many of them accumulated significant fortunes in the provinces. In the 1st century, most of their descendants moved to Rome as provincial senators.

Merchants, on the other hand, were typically plebeians or freedmen. They could normally be seen at every open-air market, in shops or at roadside stalls selling goods. Merchants also operated near Roman military camps during various campaigns in which the army was involved. They sold food and clothing to the soldiers and often paid in cash for any spoils obtained from victories on the battlefield.

In Ancient Rome, another group known as argentarii worked as agents in public or private auctions, dealing with coins. These citizens held deposits of money for other individuals, discounted checks - known as prescriptions - and acted as currency exchange houses. What is curious is that they maintained strict records, which were considered as legal evidence by the courts in case of non-payment. At times, the argentarii performed similar tasks to the mensarii, public bankers appointed by the Roman State. They received interest on loans as well as a commission fee known as merces. Some argentarii, known as coactores, collected debts and conducted auctions, while others were assisted by coactores who collected debts on their behalf.

Finally, in the 3rd century approximately, mascates were individuals who roamed the Roman Empire and comprised the smallest known itinerant commercial institutions in Antiquity. These traveling merchants carried spices and perfumes to residents in rural and remote regions far from major urban centers.

SLAVES

Slave labor played a significant role in supporting Roman commerce. These slaves were involved in the processes of production, transportation and the sale of goods. According to estimates, about half of all the slaves in Rome were owned by the upper class. Furthermore, 50% of them worked in rural areas, where they made up only a small percentage of the population, with the exception of some agricultural estates. The other half constituted a significant 25% in the cities. In these urban areas, they worked as domestic servants, prostitutes or laborers in commercial enterprises, construction and manufacturing. In conquest times, many new slaves were acquired by wholesale merchants. They were often men captured in warfare who were with the Roman armies.

According to historians, many people who bought slaves preferred strong individuals, preferably males. There is no consensus on the values of enslaved children. Some sources suggest that they had a lower cost compared to adults, while others indicate that their price could be quite high.

At the moment of a slave acquisition, they were presented naked to the prospective buyer. This was because the Romans wanted to know precisely what they were acquiring. The buyer had up to six months to return a slave if they came with any undisclosed "defect". Another option was for the merchant to provide financial compensation for the loss. Slaves who were sold without any guarantees would wear a cap during the auction.

COMMERCIAL INFRASTRUCTURE

In ancient Rome, the main commercial center was the Forum Cupedinis, which sold numerous delicacies for many years. Later, the space became better known as the Forum Magnum. This region attracted most of the commercial traffic. Originally, it was used for sporting events and as a marketplace for all imaginable goods. However, it later became the political and banking center, where negotiators, argentarii and mensarii kept their offices.

The commercial or mercantile forum - known as the Venalium - came into existence during the time of the Empire due to the rapid expansion of the city and increased business in the provinces. At least four other large markets supplied the entire region. Moreover, six smaller commercial forums were specialized in more specific products: the Forum Boarium (cattle trade), Forum Holitorium (horticultural products), Forum Suarium (pork products),

WHOLESALE

Once, the tyrant Julius Caesar supposedly sold the entire population of a conquered region in Gaul into slavery. Dealers purchased no fewer than 53 thousand people!

Forum Piscarium (fish and seafood), Forum Pistorium (various breads) and Forum Vinarium (beverages, especially wines).

The Roman Forum attracted the largest part of people traffic. Nevertheless, all places required appropriate infrastructure for both buyers and sellers to have easy access to the available goods. New cities, such as Timgad (located in modern-day Algeria), were established with an orthogonal road system that facilitated transportation and trade. The locations were connected by well--maintained roads. Navigable rivers were another widely used means of transportation, along with some dug canals. All this extensive infrastructure was discovered through archaeological excavations over time.

BY LAND AND SEA

According to the Roman historian Livy, in 752 BCE, the first Roman colonies were established. All settlements, especially smaller ones, were strategically located. Both before and after the Roman Empire, safer locations were favored for small settlements as piracy made commercial activities in coastal towns extremely dangerous.

In 67 BCE, after a battle against pirates and the consolidation of Rome's navy, under the command of Augustus, this threat was largely eradicated. On the other hand, bad weather, imprecise maps and rudimentary navigation equipment could cause significant damage to a convoy. Nevertheless, at that time, there was no better or more efficient way to transport goods than by using ships.

The type of ship commonly used by the Romans was known as the Corbita. These vessels could carry up to 600 passengers or 6,000 clay amphorae of wine, oil and similar liquids. These ships could transport more goods in a short period of time than could be moved by land. For example, a ship of this type would take between two and three weeks - depending on weather conditions - to travel from Egypt to Rome. To enhance the efficiency of maritime transportation, the Romans developed deepwater ports in key locations. One of the largest ports was in Ostia, nearly 15 miles from Rome on the Mediterranean coast. In 50 CE, a lighthouse was established there to guide navigators. At its peak, Rome placed lighthouses in 40 different locations to assist navigation.

Even before the establishment of the Republic, the Roman Kingdom was involved in regular trade using the Tiber River. The proximity to the river played a crucial role in the economic development of the city because goods arriving from the sea had to travel upstream to be directed to Etruria and to the Greek Campania.

Therefore, Rome was able to monopolize land traffic as it was situated at the intersection of major roads in inner Italy. Furthermore, due to the presence of significant saltworks near the city, Rome became a nearly perfect market point for the "Salt Road", which would later be known as the Via Salaria.

SILK ROAD

This important trade route enabled the transportation of various goods between the East and Europe. Its numerous interconnected routes through South Asia were primarily used - as the name suggests - for the silk trade. This vital passage was divided into northern and southern routes due to the presence of commercial centers at both ends of China. The Northern Silk Road crossed Eastern Europe, the Crimean Peninsula, the Black Sea, the Sea of Marmara, through the Balkans and eventually reached Italy. The southern route crossed Turkmenistan, Mesopotamia and Anatolia. At this point, it branched into routes leading to Syria or Egypt and North Africa.

The Maritime Silk Road was established between Jiaozhi (modern-day Vietnam) - controlled by the Chinese - and the Nabatean territories on the northwestern coast of the Red Sea. Most likely inaugurated in the 1st century CE, it extended along the Indian and Sri Lankan coastlines and the ports controlled by Rome, including major Egyptian ports. Merchants transported a wide variety of goods along the Silk Road.

Besides silk, gold, silver, copper, iron, lead, bronze, slaves, turtles, horses, bears, shells, ivory, amber, glass, jade, cloves, cinnamon, coriander, nutmeg, cardamom, linen, rugs, medicinal herbs, tea, jewelry, metal artifacts, wood, ceramics, porcelain and works of art. Products such as cosmetics, makeup, diamonds, pearls, coral and Western-manufactured glass traveled toward China.

The term Silk Road was coined only in the 19th century by the German scholar Ferdinand von Richthofen. It became the greatest trade

Ruins of Forum Magnum, which held, among other things, a big market

Section of the Silk Road that passes through modern-day Kazakhstan

route of all time. The secrets of silk manufacturing - which were desired by the wealthy in Europe and the Arab world - were mastered by the Chinese. That is why the fabric was chosen as a symbol of this vast overland communication network.

SAHARA

Camels played a crucial role in transporting goods across the challenging Sahara Desert. With the assistance of these resilient animals, trans--Saharan trade reached its peak initially in the 1st century BCE with the rise of the Roman Empire. In that region, goods like gold, slaves, ivory and exotic animals flowed in exchange for luxury items from the capital city of Rome.

INCENSE ROUTE

This significant trade route also connected the Eastern Kingdom to Gaza. Camel caravan routes through the Arabian deserts and ports along the southern Arabian coast were part of an extensive trade network.

Incense and myrrh, highly valued in Antiquity as perfumes, could only be obtained from trees grown in southern Arabia, Ethiopia and Somalia. Arab merchants transported not only incense and myrrh but also spices, gold, ivory, pearls, gemstones and textiles to Rome.

From the 1st century CE, good relations between the Kingdom of Meroë in Nubia and the Roman rulers of Egypt contributed to the expansion of trade across the Red Sea and the Indian Ocean.

AMBER ROUTE

Before the birth of Jesus Christ, this route already connected the North Sea and the Baltic Sea to Italy, Greece, the Black Sea and Egypt. The route remained active for many years and was important for transporting products like amber, a fossil resin widely used in the making of ornamental objects. The main river stretches were made along the Vistula and Dnieper rivers.

With the expansion of the Roman territory to the Danube, in the early 1st century under the rule of Caesar Augustus and Tiberius, the Amber Road became a Roman road within the Empire's territory. The Roman segment of the Amber Road can be found in the records of the Tabula Peutingeriana (a map that shows the network of roads in the Roman Empire). According to reports, the road provided greater security during the winter, connecting Carnuntum, on the Danube, to Aquileia, in Italy.

PROSPEROUS PROVINCES

The regions under Roman control also experienced significant economic growth during the imperial period. By the late 2nd century CE, nearly all provinces were nearly self-sufficient in mass-produced goods.

ASIA

This province was one of the most prosperous and culturally developed. The establishment of Roman rule brought a period of relative peace, which allowed the economic growth of cities like Ephesus, Pergamon, Smyrna, Sardis and Miletus.

Beautiful locations appeared not only in the southern and western parts of the peninsula but also in the central region. In all these cities, there were monumental structures such as agoras, gymnasiums, stadiums, theaters, baths, and other buildings, many of them made of marble. There were also roads paved with marble and piped water through aqueducts from sources.

HISPANIA

The presence of Rome helped the rapid economic advancement of the region. Where activities were previously more rudimentary, with the advancement of the Empire, the area began to boast an agricultural activity with efficient land use and various crops, including wheat, olive trees, fruits and vineyards. The Romans introduced commercial exchanges, encouraged currency circulation, brought wooden plows, forges, oil presses, aqueducts, roads and bridges.

Furthermore, the populations, which previously resided predominantly in the mountains, started to occupy valleys and plains. Brick houses with tiled roofs were an example of significant advancement in construction sty-

Amber has always been involved with beliefs. Many ancient peoples believed in its medicinal gift, using its powdered resin mixed with honey to combat asthma, gout and even the Black Death.

It was also present in the mystical sphere, in the fight against evil spirits. No wonder, its presence is noted in talismans, rosaries and incense to ward off bad energy.

les. Therefore, important cities like Braga, Beja, and Cacém (all within the present-day territory of Portugal) emerged.

The industry also developed, particularly pottery, mining, weaving and quarries, which substantially expanded trade, now taking place in fairs and markets. All this structure was supported by a vast network of roads.

BRITAIN

Its natural wealth was one of the main reasons for Rome's conquest. The region was rich in substantial quantities of tin and iron. Silver and gold were also prevalent there, which was significant in supplying Rome, as the mines in Hispania were nearly depleted.

In the plains, both cities and farms were well integrated into the mercantile economy. London and other ancient cities in Britain developed and thrived during the first two centuries of Roman administration. They exported gold, silver, iron, tin, grains, meat and wool.

From the time when the border limits were fortified in Britain, under the emperors Hadrian (117-138 CE) and Antoninus Pius (138-161 CE), a space of prosperous economic activity emerged south of the frontier wall. Investors extracted lead, silver, iron and salt from there.

MACEDONIA

In this province, the economy was significantly stimulated by the construction of the Via Egnatia – a road built by the Romans in the 2nd century BCE –, by the arrival of merchants in cities and by the foundation of Roman colonies. With rich arable pastures, dominant families amassed significant wealth through slave labor.

The improvement in living conditions for the productive classes increased the number of artisans in the province. Stonemasons, miners and blacksmiths were employed in various commercial and artisanal activities.

The export economy was essentially based on agriculture and livestock. Iron, copper and gold, along with products like wood, resin, pitch, linen, hemp and fish were also widely exported. Ports such as Dion, Pella and Thessalonica experienced significant growth during the Roman period.

EGYPT

With much prestige, the Egyptian province was of paramount importance to Rome. And it was no wonder since it supplied the wheat needed for the capital and was an easily defensible location against external attacks. In addition to wheat, there were abundant vineyards for the production of wine in large amounts. Furthermore, Roman emperors still held a monopoly over the mines, salt pans and papyrus production.

Before the discovery of the monsoon winds from the Indian Ocean – a periodic climatic occurrence that benefits agricultural activities –, Alexandria became the center of trade between the East and the West and the second most important city in the Roman Empire (second only, of course, to Rome). Alexandria served as a major warehouse, receiving and exporting Egypt's products and exotic materials from India and the East, brought during the monsoon seasons to the ports of the Red Sea and transported to the Nile across the desert.

SYRIA

This was another region that prospered greatly with the advent of Roman rule. Syria abundantly exported resin, wood, ceramics, linen, wool, cloth, grains, fruits and, especially, dyes. The purple dye, extracted from mollusks on the Syrian coast, held particular value. Ports and trade routes with the Far East played a significant role in the local economy.

Cities like Aleppo, Antioch, Palmyra and Damascus became extremely wealthy through the trade of silks, cedar wood, perfumes, jewelry, wines and spices. They grew so much that they became the primary commercial centers of Roman Syria.

GERMANIA

Located on the banks of the Rhine River, it quickly became an important Roman trading center north of the Alps. Even today, there are still some traces of that period, such as parts of the Roman wall, some of the gates and the aqueduct. The city map of Cologne still reflects the network of streets and avenues from the Roman era.

In those fields, more profitable cereal varieties were cultivated and larger breeds of cattle and horses were raised. Vineyards extended across the regions of the Rhine, Mosel and Neckar. Practically all types of fruits we know today, such as cherries and pears, were harvested there. Likewise, asparagus, celery and chard were also cultivated in those lands. By the end of the Roman rule, the number of edible plants in southern Germany had doubled.

AFRICA PROCONSULARIS

Farming in this region became a highly profitable endeavor. In the first century, the fertile land south of Carthage already produced significant amounts of wheat. By the following century, crops had diversified, and olive groves became a good source of profit. Furthermore, orchards and vineyards contributed to the economy of Proconsular Africa. Livestock also played a vital economic role, including sheep and cattle, goats and horses. These livestock ventures guaranteed excellent profits.

Roads were crucial for agricultural advancement, as they allowed products to be easily transported to city markets. In terms of the Empire, these roads enabled a significant export industry to work. In renowned ports like Carthage, ships departed for Rome loaded with wheat, ceramics, marble and other valuable goods.

ITALY

The locality had greater success in growing corn, wheat, barley, olives and grapes. In central Italy, household utensils were manufactured to equip the Roman army in Gaul and Germany. These items were traded beyond the borders of the empire, in Britain and northern Europe.

In the early Christian era, the pottery trade, whose main production center was Arezzo, Italy, supplied the Roman market as well as the western, northern and southeastern provinces of the Empire.

JUDEA

Due to its strategic position, Judea was a transit region where soldiers, traders, messengers and even diplomats passed. The region had important urban centers like Caesarea Maritima, Gaza and Jerusalem, which attracted people and economic activities. Just like in other parts of the Empire, there were roads and ports in this region, facilitating the transportation of goods and communication.

Trade was widely practiced. Internally, local exchanges took place aiming at simply supplying the major cities. Judea, in turn, imported luxury products - consumed by the upper classes and the Temple - and exported food (fruits, wines, oil and fish) and manufactured goods (perfumes and bitumen).

ACHAIA

The region belonging to Greece had a rather complex system of industry and trade for those times. A significant portion of raw materials, such as lead, copper and iron, was available in Achaia. Among agricultural items, the most important imports included honey, olives, olive oil and wine.

Practically every luxury domestic item was crafted in Achaia. Pre-

Ruins of Alexandria, trade center between East and West

cious oils, powders, perfumes, cosmetics, clothing, ceramics, dyes, furniture and many other products were manufactured in Greek factories and workshops. Sculptures and other works of art were also widely exported to the Roman world.

GAUL

Under the Roman Empire, the region enjoyed significant prosperity. In the 1st and 2nd centuries CE, Gaul advanced economically through the export of meat, grains, wine, silver, glass and ceramics. Some cities, such as Arles, Narbonne, and Trier became significantly wealthier.

Grains were cultivated in the plains of the Paris Basin and modern-day Belgium. Flax and hemp were also grown for the production of the famous Gaulish textiles. To these traditional resources, the Romans added vineyard culture, which was introduced in the northern regions.

ARABIA PETRAEA

This was another region that prospered during the Roman Empire's rule. Petra, one of the most important cities in the area, primarily traded in incense, spices and textiles.

The Roman conquest of Arabia was a significant victory both in terms of commerce and military control. The Romans had complete control over all accessible and important trade routes in the Mediterranean. Another benefit of the addition of Arabia was that the Romans secured the southern flank of the provinces of Syria and Judea.

BITHYNIA

Located in a fertile plain, the province harvested grains abundantly. A constant flow of goods passed through its ports. Its main cities were Nicaea, Prusa and Nicomedia.

MOESIA

This region, in addition to acting as a sort of buffer between the Greek provinces and various potential invaders, also had rich mines and very fertile fields.

DACIA

The main activities in the province were agriculture, viniculture, livestock breeding and metalwork. The inhabitants of Dacia had large herds, not only of cattle but also of sheep. They were well-known for beekeeping outside the region. Dacian horses were highly esteemed and sought after for military use. The Romans had control over the gold and silver mines in Transylvania. The province also maintained a considerable external market, as evidenced by the various foreign coins found in the country

PANNONIA

It was a very productive location. Oats and barley were its main agricultural products. On the other hand, vineyards and olive trees were cultivated in small quantities. Timber was one of its most important exports. Iron and silver mining also prevailed. Additionally, the province of Pannonia was famous for its breed of hunting dogs.

ECONOMIC DECLINE

There is no simple reason to explain with all the necessary accuracy the financial decline of the Roman Empire over the years. One of the reasons might have been the sharp decrease in the number of slaves. By the 3rd century, without major military campaigns that would secure new lands and free labor, the situation had reached a near-definitive shortage of slaves. Thus, the effect of the slave system's crisis also led to an economic decline, with high prices for various items and shortage of products in practically all cities.

Along with the economic crisis, there came a disruption in the production structures due to the continuous administrative taxes increase, massive bourgeois expenses on housing in urban centers, currency devaluation, worsening living conditions for the lower classes, rising product costs and the replacement of monetary payments with payments in kind, which led to the decline of trade.

There was also a systematic increase in agricultural product imports, which meant a higher outflow of coins from the Empire, exacerbated by the fact that precious metal mines were already exhausted by that time.

The sum of all these elements, as well as the growing insecurity of trade routes, generated a severe financial crisis, which in turn caused the decline of trade and all urban activity. To make matters worse, according to the historian Pliny, the constant importation of goods from the East, and the almost complete lack of exports to that same region as a counterpart created a huge deficit in the Roman government's accounts. Thus, it became impossible to keep that large amount of expenses for two centuries.

The debt with foreign countries led to a depletion of cash. The monetary reform carried out by Emperor Diocletian, between the 3rd and 4th centuries, attempted to reverse this situation but did not last long, as it significantly affected production.

Within this complicated context, the successive political crises that occurred from the end of the reign of Marcus Aurelius until Diocletian, with their successive civil wars, barbarian invasions, epidemics and confiscations led to a tragic economic decline, with the disappearance of cash, the collapse of major trading activities and a return to the so--called natural economy. Rome had reached an economic condition that rendered any rule or law impotent and ineffective. In the 3rd and 4th centuries, the Roman Empire was unable to provide for its population, maintain its administration and pay its troops.

Eventually, Rome became an idle capital. The free distribution of grain to Roman proletarians reached 200,000 poor people at a certain point. This free distribution in Egypt, Sicily and Proconsular Africa was offset by the money Rome drained from the provinces. Roman trade was based on indirect exploitation – it repaid imports with the taxes it imposed on the provinces. The sad reality is that Rome turned into a city of beggars.

Ensuring the minimum sustenance for the population became a political necessity after the rule of Caesar. In addition to the free grain distributions, games were one of the most important public services of the State. So, the number of holidays increased from 65 in Caesar's time to 135 in Marcus Aurelius's time. Later, it went up to 175 days. From that time, the population of Rome spent their lives in theaters, amphitheaters and the circus.

Facing a less-than-optimistic scenario, there was little left to do but remember the golden days of a true economic power.

9

THE ROMAN WAY

ETERNAL VALUES AND POLITICAL INTERESTS EXPLAIN PART OF THE BEHAVIOR OF THIS EPOCH-MAKING SOCIETY

At the beginning of the Roman civilization, its members led lives considered rather simple. They were field workers and carried out subsistence agriculture, that is, they planted and harvested only what was essential for survival. Discipline and modesty, in fact, were evaluated as essential virtues for a man.

Family, on the other hand, was regarded as a sacred institution, and its head - pater familias - had complete power, authority and unlimited rights over his wife, children, slaves and other material possessions. Furthermore, great respect was held for the elderly, who served as examples to be followed by the community at large.

Religion, in turn, was based on the cult of ancestors and the worship of a multitude of gods. Religious practice permeated various aspects of daily life and had a civic character, as it was directly linked to the Roman State.

Time intertwined the tradition of the Greek gods with that of the Romans due to the significant influence of Greece - one of the provinces of the Empire - on the culture of the peoples of that historical period.

The Roman citizens also placed the State above all else. Those who served the res publica (public thing) were required to respect the gods, demonstrate loyalty and courage, as well as aspire to glory. These qualities underscored the warrior character manifested through time among Romans.

Ruins of the temple of Apollo, one of the gods worshiped by the Roman civilization

THE PRINCIPLE OF EVERYTHING

In general, the inhabitants of Rome believed they could and should live under obligations to both the gods and other people. They also understood that respect in society was earned or lost based on an individual's behavior. This was the mindset of the majority and not of everyone, as there were always exceptions within certain groups. This line of thinking also evolved significantly over the years.

Nevertheless, some things did not change. In addition to holding political power, the upper class was also responsible for defining the moral values that guided the public and private life of Romans around 500 BCE, during the Republican Era. To prevent a single ruler from governing, members of the social elite established the republican system by creating a principle of power-sharing among themselves, but not for all citizens. Hence, they intended to take power out of the hands of the majority because they firmly believed that the poorer citizens might prefer to live under the rule of a king who could gain their support through financial benefits. They believed the wealthy would be forced to provide these benefits from their personal fortunes.

On the other hand, since the upper class was too small to manage and defend Rome on its own, they needed to make concessions, such as granting some governmental roles to citizens of lower social and financial status. Without such pacts, the Romans would not have been able to, among other things, organize a strong army. The Roman Republican Era was marked by intense struggles for power. The bloodiest battle occurred during the Late Republic, when the upper class engaged in legendary conflicts among themselves to determine who would attain specific government positions.

Many historians question whether this relentless pursuit of power, which made citizens struggle against each other, had its roots in the Romans' failure to follow traditional values. According to Harvard University professor Thomas R. Martin, this destructive scenario seems to have been caused "by some tension stemming from the overwhelming importance the Romans placed on achieving individual status as a reward for service to the community".

The people of Rome believed that their ancestors, over time, had passed down the values that should guide their entire lives. As a result, they often referred to the value system as "the custom of the ancestors".

VALUES

Probity, fidelity and status. These were the three core values the Romans believed had been established by their ancestors. The first one, essentially, defined how a person related to their peers. Initially, probity had a masculine sense and derived from the Latin virtus, which means virtue. The poet Lucilius listed what he considered to be the moral qualities of a virtuous man: someone who could distinguish between good and evil, who knew how to recognize what was useless, who was against wicked men, who was a protector of the good people and who put the well-being of the nation first, followed by family interests, and lastly, personal interests.

Furthermore, it was the duty of a man of probity to take good care of his body and exercise to stay healthy and strong in order to support his family and fight for the country in times of war. The ultimate achievement for the just man was heroism in battle, but only if it served the community rather than providing personal glory. Women of probity were expected to perform valiant actions for their families. Above all, they were supposed to marry, have children and raise them from a young age according to the ethical principles of the community in which they lived.

The value of fidelity took on various forms. Above all, such loyalty meant the fulfillment of obligations without considering the price to be paid or even whether the commitment was informal or formal. For a native of Rome, failing to meet an obligation or completely disregarding a contract was a great offense to the community and also to their gods. For women, for instance, fidelity was demonstrated by remaining a virgin until the wedding and, in marriage, being a monogamous wife – having a relationship only with their husband. However, the same standard did not apply to men, as sexual acts with prostitutes were not considered a matter of public reproach. For Roman men, what truly mattered was keeping their word, paying debts properly and treating all people with a sense of justice.

Lastly, status – the third central Roman value – was nothing but the reward one achieved for living according to all these values. This came from the respect a person earned and also expected from others for behaving correctly concerning traditional commitments. Women gained respect – along with rewards related to their reputation and social acceptance – when they bore legitimate children and raised them with moral principles. Roman mothers, in fact, deserved and expected great respect.

The rewards for men involved public honors. In other words, elections to official positions in the State – for those wealthy enough to enter the government, as they did not receive a salary. As for soldiers in the citizen militia of Rome, they expected public recognition for their acts of courage. According to historians, the influence of social status was so profound that a man with an extremely high reputation for his actions and self-control could receive so much respect that everyone else would obey him, even without legal or formal authority. It was often said that someone who reached this pinnacle of prestige had moral authority. This meant that people

PIETY

For the Romans, being pious meant devotion to the worship of the gods and to the support of one's household. Besides the religious nature, this value was also social. Men and women who followed this precept used to respect the authority of their elders, family ancestors and also deities. In fact, showing respect to the gods – performing religious services properly and regularly – was essential. It is worth mentioning that divine favor, according to the Romans, guaranteed the protection of their community.

It did not mean that self-respect was absent from the values of a pious person. That is because self-respect meant many other things. It meant, above all, that man should never give up, regardless of the difficulties he might face. Persevering and fulfilling duties under all conditions – no matter how adverse – were basic behaviors. Self-respect, finally, also meant limiting expressions of emotion and always maintaining self-control. The expectation regarding this aspect was so great that not even husbands and wives were allowed to kiss in public to avoid conveying the feeling of having lost emotional control.

would do what he recommended not because of legal enforcement but due to the immense respect they had for the supreme example of living according to the values passed down by their ancestors.

WEALTH

The inhabitants of Ancient Rome believed that family status directly influenced values. For them, the higher a person's family class, the more strict the personal values should be. Within this Roman line of thinking, being born into a prominent household had both pros and cons. On the one hand, it guaranteed a higher status in society. On the other hand, it imposed a stricter standard for behavior evaluation. In general, members of the elite believed that a person born into a disreputable family also had a lesser ability to behave properly. This view often created tension between social classes. In theory, wealth had no direct relation to moral virtue. The Romans themselves would often tell their children stories about fellow countrymen who were poor but highly virtuous heroes.

However, as Rome expanded over the centuries, conquering new lands and extending its dominion, money began to hold greater significance for the elite. It had the power to elevate one's status through extravagant spending on public buildings and entertainment for the surrounding community. Thus, having money became a necessity for those who sought to ascend in social prestige. In the 2nd century BCE, more ambitious Romans needed financial resources to buy respect, and as a result, there was a significant increase in the willingness to disregard other values to achieve this goal. The pursuit of certain "values" would eventually lead Rome into a period of unrest and, during the Late Republic (146 BCE to 27 BCE), into a state of dictatorship.

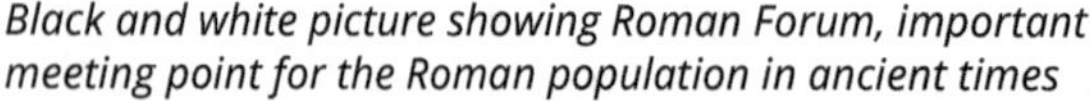

Black and white picture showing Roman Forum, important meeting point for the Roman population in ancient times

PATRON AND CLIENT

The republican environment brought about a new relationship: that of patron and client. In reality, they both formed a network of reciprocal obligations. The patron was a man of higher social status whose responsibility was to provide "kindness" to those of lower status. These benefited individuals, in turn, became clients and owed "tasks" to the patron. It is important to note that even patrons, for instance, could be clients of people with higher status than themselves. In other words, one individual could be both a patron and a client.

Romans often described this relationship of mutual interests as a kind of friendship in which each party had their roles precisely defined. For example, a sensitive patron would show respect to the client by addressing them as "my friend" rather than "my client".

However, despite this seemingly friendly and respectful air, this patron-client relationship was legally supported and guaranteed rights and duties for those involved. The Law of the Twelve Tables, established in 449 BCE, which was the first set of written rules in Rome, declared it a crime for a patron to deceive their client.

The duties of a client included providing financial and political support to the patron. According to tradition, a client was expected to assist, for example, in providing dowries – very valuable wedding gifts – for the daughters of the patron. In political life, a client was expected to help their patron in campaigns for public offices or when a friend of the patron was running for election. The client was very useful in persuading people to change their votes. They could also be called upon to lend money to the patron when they had won an election and needed financial resources to fund the expected public works.

In the Late Republic, it was common and prestigious for a patron to have a large number of clients at all times. The interesting thing is that these various clients would often gather at the patron's house early in the morning and accompany them to the Roman Forum – the commercial, political and legal center of Rome. Therefore, a member of the Roman elite needed to have a large and opulent home to host such a morning assembly. Additionally, it was a good practice for the patron to invite this social partner to dinners in their own residence. Having a lot of people around was a sign of social success. Given this scenario, money became crucial for the Roman upper classes. They had to spend large sums to be seen as excellent patrons.

Not only that. Generally, the patron had to spend money to offer a variety of costly favors to their clients in this "two-way street". In the republican system, it was considered in good form for a patron to assist a client in starting a political career by supporting their candidacy for office or by providing occasional financial support. During the Empire, the patron was expected to offer a basket of food for the breakfast of clients who were in their house early in the morning.

However, the most important obligation of the patron was to ensure the livelihood of the client and their family in legal difficulties, such as legal actions related to ownership and property, which were quite common. In such situations, people of lower social status were at a disadvantage in the Roman judicial system if they did not have influential friends to assist them in presenting their causes. The help of a patron with eloquence was a specific need in court, as accusers and accused had to speak for themselves or have close associates speak on their behalf.

In this historical period, Rome did not have - as it does today - public prosecutors or defense attorneys provided by the State, nor private defense lawyers for hire. Hence, prominent citizens with more knowledge of history and legal procedures were the legal experts in that region. In the 3rd century BCE, these self-taught experts, known as jurists, played a crucial role in the judicial system.

All the reciprocal legal obligations of the patron-client relationship were meant to be stable and enduring. In certain situations, these bonds extended across generations and became a part of the family. An example was a former slave who automatically became a lifelong client of the master who had freed them and often this client passed on to their children this relationship with the patron's family. Romans with connections beyond the borders could acquire foreign clients. Especially the wealthiest had, in some cases, entire communities of clients.

The characteristics of duty and permanence in the patron-client system reflected the Roman idea that stability and social well-being were achieved through the faithful maintenance of a network of connections that brought people together in both public and private lives.

FAMILY

Roman legislation made paternal power the dominant force within family relationships, with the exception of the bond between husband and wife. The granting of authority to older men made Rome a patriarchal society. A father had legal power over his children - regardless of their age - and over his slaves, who were considered members of his household.

This paternal power also made the head of the family the sole owner of all the land acquired by any of his children. As long as the father was alive, no son or daughter could, legally, have anything in their name. However, in practice, adult children often maintained personal property and obtained financial resources. Similarly, protected slaves could have their own savings.

The father also had legal authority over the life and death of those under his roof. Yet, it was quite rare for him to exercise this right over anyone. As for the abandonment of newborns, it was quite common. It was an accepted practice to control family size and discard children born with various physical problems.

In the wife's case, paternal power had a much more limited effect on her life. In the early days of the Republic, a woman could be under the authority of her husband. However, the marriage contract could include specific impediments to her subjection, freeing her from any legal control by the man. In such cases, the wife remained, in theory, under the power of her father as long as he was alive. Nevertheless, there were few cases of elderly fathers maintaining control over the lives of mature, married daughters, as most people died young in the ancient world. When Roman women got married, at the end of their adolescence mostly, practically half of them had already lost their fathers. This demographic reality shows that paternal power had a very limited effect on older children.

Furthermore, adult women without a living father also had full autonomy. Regarding men, since they did not marry before the age of 30, at the time of marriage and the formation of their own families, only 20% of them still had a living father. Thus, the other 80% were legally independent of paternal control.

WOMEN

Normally, Roman society expected a woman to develop quickly and to assume her responsibilities within the family. Tullia (79 BCE to 45 BCE), daughter of the famous politician and orator Cicero, became engaged at the age of 12, married at 16 and became a widow at just 22. Wealthy women had the duty of managing their family's property, including the household slaves.

Wives also had the responsibility of overseeing the upbringing of their children by nursemaids and being present alongside their husbands at festive dinners, which were very important to form relationships between families.

The influence of the mother in shaping the moral character of her children held special value in Roman society. An example was Cornelia, an affluent member of the upper class in the 2nd century BCE, who gained fame and respect for managing her family's property and for educating her children. When her husband died, she decided to decline a marriage proposal from the King of Egypt to oversee the family's estate and educate a daughter and two sons - Tiberius and Gaius Gracchus, who grew up among some of the most influential and controversial political leaders of the Republican Period.

On the other hand, poor women had to raise their children and had to work hard to support themselves. The number of professions open to women was limited. Typically, women had to accept jobs related to selling products or food in small shops. Even if they belonged to a family involved in craftsmanship - which was prevalent in the Roman economy - women were more likely to be involved in selling the products rather than manufacturing them.

Women from poorer families would often turn to prostitution to make a living. Prostitution was legal, but those who earned a living by selling their bodies were considered to have no social status. Prostitutes would wear a piece of male clothing - the toga - to signal their lack of traditional chastity associated with Roman heroines.

Women were not allowed to vote in Roman elections, nor could they hold public office. They could only exert indirect political influence by expressing their opinions to relatives in public office. Marcus Porcius Cato, an eminent senator and author (234 BCE to 149 BCE), once humorously described the influence women could exercise over their governing husbands: "The whole world rules their wives, we rule the whole world and our wives rule us".

SEX

The sexual conduct of the ancient Romans may seem highly immoral for today's standards. For example, citizens of ancient Rome could take advantage of the intimacy of their slaves, both female and young male slaves. Adopted children - treated as if they were one's own - were often subject to homosexual practices. Relationships between an adult and an adolescent were allowed, but never between two adult men.

However, sexual intercourse with one's wife was typically in the dark, and her breast was covered with a kind of bra, never to be revealed. Romans were puritanical in this aspect, but they adorned their homes with paintings and mosaics depicting nudes and erotic motifs, especially in bedrooms.

In the Roman Empire, such as in Ancient Greece, prostitution was not forbidden and was often carried out by slaves brought from other places, Greek and Eastern women. Although people knew that there were rooms designated for sexual encounters in taverns, excavations in the ruins of Pompeii found a single brothel consisting of ten rooms. These establishments were referred to as Lupanare, a word derived from lupae, prostitutes who frequented public parks and attracted clients with wolf-like howls.

Lesbianism was also allowed in ancient Rome. In public baths, it was common for women, even if they were married, to seek out female slaves to satisfy their deeper lesbian desires.

EDUCATION

An important point to note is that Roman education for children was private for both the rich and the poor as there were no public schools. When adults from poorer families – who often worked as producers of goods - knew how to read, write and do arithmetic, they typically passed on this knowledge to their children through informal homeschooling. Since Rome had no laws prohibiting or limiting child labor, these children would engage in paid work alongside their parents.

Nonetheless, it is highly likely that the vast majority of the population could not read or write. Children from wealthier Roman families would also receive basic education within their own homes.

In the early days of the republican government, parents were responsible for their children's education until they reached the age of 7. After that age, children were considered ready to receive instruction from a hired tutor. Children could also attend classes offered by independent teachers for a fee.

Parents aimed to instill their children with the foundations of male virtue, especially physical training, combat with weapons, and courage. When Roman expansion brought the wealthier individuals into contact with Greek culture, they started to purchase educated Greek slaves to educate their children. Many of these children became bilingual in Latin and Greek.

Girls usually received milder training compared to boys, but both sexes learned to read among the upper-class citizens. Repetition was the standard teaching technique. Physical punishment was used to

FEMALE MANIFESTATION

It was quite rare for women to engage in any acts of political nature. However, in 215 BCE, at the height of a wartime financial crisis, a law was approved limiting the amount of gold women could have, prohibiting them from wearing colorful clothing in public and riding in carriages within a distance of 1 mile from Rome or other Roman municipalities, except for attending religious events.

This law aimed to address the dissatisfaction of men regarding the resources controlled by wealthy women during a time when the State was facing a significant need for funds. In 195 BCE, after the war, women affected by the rule organized a large demonstration against the restrictions imposed. They took to the streets to express what they wanted and surrounded the doors of the homes of two political leaders who had been trying to block the repeal of the rule. Faced with pressure, the law was annulled.

keep students focused on routine work. Wealthy families provided their daughters with instruction in literature, a bit of music and conversational topics for social occasions and festive dinners.

One of the primary goals of female education was to prepare them for the role of Roman mothers. That is, they needed to know how to teach their children about the moral and social values of Rome. The aim of educating a high-class Roman boy was to turn him into an expert in rhetoric, as this was crucial for a successful public career. To be elected, a man needed to be able to speak persuasively to his voters. Additionally, speaking effectively in the courts was essential since legal actions were a means of protecting private property.

A boy would learn rhetorical techniques by attending public meetings, assemblies and court sessions with his father, uncle or older brother. By listening to speeches on political debates and legal matters, the boy learned to imitate winning techniques. Moreover, wealthy parents would hire teachers capable of conveying a wide range of knowledge in History, Geography, Literature and Finance - disciplines necessary to form a truly effective orator.

Roman rhetoric owed much to the techniques of Greek rhetoric, and many Roman orators studied with Greek teachers.

DAILY LIFE

It is believed that the Romans used to wake at sunrise since the streets had no lighting and households had only oil lamps. They would wash their faces and immediately put on their sandals or wooden shoes. They did not waste time changing their clothing, as they usually slept in their everyday attire (or wearing several tunics layered, depending on the time of year).

After that, they would have their first meal of the day: bread, cheese and water. Young boys from wealthy families would then head to their studies escorted by trusted slaves.

The rich used the morning period to attend to their business, visit their properties and handle other personal matters. Strolling through the forum (public square) to get to know the latest news, discuss public affairs and socialize with friends was a common activity.

Around noon, the Romans would pause for their second meal, which was quick and typically consisted of cold meats, fruits, and vegetables, all combined with a good wine. After eating, they would return to their work, usually stopping in the mid-afternoon for bathing.

The day was concluded with the main meal, dinner. The wealthy often liked to invite friends to their banquets. They would have multiple courses served by slaves on common platters, from which guests would take their food using spoons or even their hands. After the banquet, they enjoyed entertainment such as musicians, dancers or poetry recitals.

For the poorer Romans, work continued into the evening and their dinner was simple, based on wheat - which was often distributed for free or at a low cost, especially during the imperial period. They would sleep early and wake up at sunrise to start another day of work.

STANDARDIZED CLOTHING

The clothing of Rome's inhabitants was greatly influenced by the Greeks and varied depending on gender and social status. Unmarried women, for instance, typically wore a sleeveless tunic that extended to the ankle. After marriage, they wore the same type of garment but with sleeves. The sort of fabric also differed. Elite women dressed in cotton and silk, while those from less privileged classes wore linen or wool.

Free men, on the other hand, wore knee-length tunics made of linen or wool. This length prevented the garments from hindering their movements. Laborers, however, wore leather clothing for its durability. The toga, a long mantle, was worn only by citizens from the age of 14. Boys wore a shell-shaped ornament around their neck, which was discarded when they donned the toga, symbolizing their arrival into adulthood.

Accessories also played a significant role in Roman attire. Women often wore bracelets, anklets, wristbands, rings and necklaces. Common jewelry materials included gold, silver, precious and semi-precious stones, as well as metals like copper, bronze and iron. These pieces often featured symbols like the Cupid, birds, and mythological scenes.

Romans also used makeup and wigs to enhance their appearance. To complete their attire, men preferred sandals, slippers, and boots made of felt or leather.

Over time, there were, of course, some changes and additions, such as an under-tunic worn beneath the main garment. This new piece featured a distinctive hood

END OF ANCIENT CUSTOMS

The main principles established over the years in Rome ended up deteriorating over time. The unrestrained pursuit of power and financial resources led many leaders and members of the upper classes to distort values long practiced in Roman territory.

Insane behaviors of emperors such as Caligula (37 to 41 CE) and Nero (54 to 68 CE) – who sought their own glory above all else – are examples. A clear proof of this is that, for both of them, there was no longer the need to respect the opinions of the elders, something established as essential.

Other emperors who came later partly returned to some of the essential values, but much had already changed. Rome would not return to the same customs, and for that reason, a period of decline as the dominant nation it once was had begun. The tyrannical actions of some in the past would ultimately dilute Roman prosperity in the future.

10

GREEK AND ETRUSCAN INFLUENCES ON THE SCENE

TERRITORIAL RULERS, THE ROMANS WERE COMPLETELY CHARMED BY THE GREEK ARTISTS IN ANCIENT TIMES; ETRURIA ALSO INTERFERED DIRECTLY IN THE ROMAN ART

The territory controlled spanned from Gaul to Carthage, from Greece to Egypt. However, not even their unmatched military power and victorious military campaigns could prevent Rome from succumbing to something: Greek art. Actually, it is true that virtually everything artistically produced by the Romans during their golden years was influenced by this province.

For many historians, in fact, the "Eternal City" – as the capital of the ancient Empire came to be known – produced very little original art. According to experts, the Romans "suppressed" the only significant artistic expression found on Italian soil, which was Etruscan. Instead of celebrating their internal content, they preferred to import Greek sculptors, decorators, and painters. Some critics point out that powerful Rome contributed less to art than small states, such as Sumeria, for example.

On the other hand, other experts reject this view. For them, Roman society was highly cosmopolitan and open, which allowed for the incorporation of certain Greek elements. However, they argue that we cannot say in any way that Roman art was a mere copy. They cite, as its main characteristics, the idea of energy, strength, realism, and material grandeur.

BEGINNING

At the beginning of the 1st century BCE, Gaius Maecenas, advisor to Emperor Augustus, was the first of the prominent patrons of local art. In his time, artists achieved, for the first time in Roman society, the same prestige as soldiers and politicians.

Still, the origins of Roman art itself date back to around the 8th century BCE. In the 4th century CE, this artistic movement on the Italian peninsula came to an end to make way for early Christian art.

Artistic creations in Rome, especially in architecture and the plastic arts, achieved remarkable unity as a result of the political power that extended across the vast Empire. Roman civilization gave rise to great cities. The military structure favored defensive constructions - such as fortresses and walls - as well as public works (roads, aqueducts, and bridges). The high degree of organization in that society and the utilitarian nature of their way of life were the main factors that characterized their artistic production during this period.

ARCHITECTURE

One of the high points of Roman art was the grandeur of its constructions. With the power it wielded in its time, this idea extended to the majestic buildings, especially in the capital of the Empire. Even based on Greek foundations, there is no denying the competence developed by Rome in executing its architecture. For this reason, some say that it was in civil engineering that the Romans truly excelled.

It is important to note that these constructions were undertaken within a context of expansion. Buildings were constructed according to the development of cities. Therefore, practicality often took precedence over

Bridge over Tiber River is an example of the utilitarianism of the Roman art

architectural effect. The beauty of their works stemmed from this functional character.

In general, Roman architects used Greek forms but developed new construction techniques, such as the arch, which spans a greater distance than the Greek system of pillar and lintel – two vertical posts supporting a horizontal beam. Concrete allowed for more flexible designs, like vaulted ceilings and immense circular areas with a dome-supported high roof.

It was precisely this functional aspect that led the Romans to develop the arch, vault, and dome, elements not used by the Greeks, although they were aware of them. However, the Romans, with their need to conquer space, made extensive use of arches since they enabled the construction of grand and expansive buildings.

Concerning Roman architecture, it is impossible to ignore the most famous of these structures, the Colosseum – the enormous arena for 50 thousand spectators where the population was entertained by the emperors with large-scale spectacles. According to the 20th-century art historian Ernst Gombrich, the Colosseum clearly exhibits characteristics of Roman construction that garnered much admiration in subsequent times.

URBANISM

Contemporary knowledge of ancient Roman architecture comes from various archaeological excavations conducted throughout the area of the Empire, as well as from written records, such as dedications, books, and inscriptions.

Following the Etruscan plan, the Romans built their cities around two main avenues, one running north to south and the other from east to west, with a square (or forum) at their intersection. Public buildings were typically grouped around the forum.

Roman architecture - initially dominated by Etruscan influence - developed its own style with the emergence of cement in the 2nd century BCE, the use of bricks and the refinement of arches. The constructions from the last two centuries of the Empire are among the most significant expressions of Roman art.

After the great fire occurred in Nero's reign, the urban landscape was transformed by reconstructions. The grand imperial forums, including the most magnificent of all, Trajan's Forum, can be highlighted here. Trajan's Forum featured the "markets", consisting of six stories of shops connected by corridors and staircases, carved into the living rock of the Quirinal Hill. A true masterpiece of Roman engineering and architecture with its roots in the East, Trajan's Forum was surrounded by a massive wall adorned with marble and included meeting rooms, libraries, a temple dedicated to Trajan and a basilica.

The creation of thermal baths was an original Roman innovation. In major cities, they occupied significant space, featuring baths, saunas and numerous attached facilities. The Baths of Agrippa in Rome, now disappeared, represent the first example of the monumental concept of Roman baths from the 2nd and 3rd centuries. Among the most famous are the Baths of Emperor Caracalla - which included libraries, reading and conversation rooms, gymnasiums and a theater - and those of Diocletian, the largest of all, covering an incredible area of 1,506,000 square feet.

In 50 BCE, Pompey constructed the first masonry theater, replacing wood. Unlike the Greeks, Roman theaters had a semicircular space reserved for the audience, a small orchestra - for dances, musicians and choirs - and a larger stage with a masonry background.

The mausoleum, a type of tomb, became prevalent during the reign of Augustus. From the older temples, only a few remnants were left, such as the temples of Jupiter Capitolinus, Saturn and Ceres, all in Rome. From the 1st century onwards, there was a significant influence from Syria, characterized by the immense wealth of decorative elements.

SCULPTURE

The influence of Etruscan art is evident in Roman sculpture until the 2nd century BCE, despite the scarcity of remaining artifacts. After this historical period, the Hellenistic style became predominant. With their dominance over Greek territory, Rome acquired numerous pieces from Greek sanctuaries in southern Italy and Anatolia. Later, Greek artists residing in the capital of the Empire created replicas and imitations of highly esteemed Greek works.

In general, the names of the artists are not known, and even important works, such as the "Altar of Augustan Peace", remained anonymous. Romans were averse to the athletic nudity of Greek sculpture, which partly explains the absence of anatomical studies in this art. The face was the most important part of their sculptures.

Hence, Roman sculpture gradually developed its distinctive style. While architecture is often considered the greatest Roman achievement, it is important to note that they created a characteristic style of sculpture as well. The most notable examples are the famous Roman busts, which have garnered the attention of art enthusiasts. In this case, it was no longer the gods being worshiped, even though the portrayed figures had striking similarities to divinities.

Later, during the Roman Empire, emperors were preserved in busts and statues, objects that were viewed with a certain reverence. However, these portraits were more realistic and perhaps less satisfactory than Greek works. Roman artists aimed to represent their subjects faithfully, but they did not see them as perfect and sublime gods, as their sculpture was more literal. This practical spirit of the Romans led them toward reality. Thus, the realm of imagination - emphasized by the Greeks - gradually lost its prominence.

According to Agnes Strickland, "the Romans had wax masks of their ancestors at home". The historian points out that these realistic images were entirely factual molds of the deceased person's features, and this tradition influenced other Roman sculptors.

Apart from busts and statues, narrative reliefs played a crucial role. Panels of sculpted figures depicting military achievements adorned triumphal arches, under which victorious armies paraded with long lines of chained prisoners.

According to the art historian Ernst Gombrich, Trajan's Column, for instance, depicts a fully illustrated chronicle of his wars and victories in Dacia - modern-day Romania. All the ingenuity and achievements of centuries of Greek art were used in these authentic feats of war reporting. However, the Romans placed great importance on the exact reproduction of details and a clear narrative that would record the achievements of a campaign - impressing those who stayed home - which altered the character of the art.

While the panels were well-crafted, the Romans' goal was the perfect illustration of a historical event. They no longer concerned themselves with ideals of beauty or harmony in their works as the Greeks did. They had a refined taste for narration. The subjects which were narrated and represented became the most important element of all.

Sculpture flourished in the 1st and 2nd centuries, particularly during the reign of Hadrian, under strong Greek influence. A second important phase began in 193 CE with Septimius Severus. However, the turbulent political conditions from the 3rd century onward led to the decline of all the arts, including sculpture. Among domestic objects (such as lamps, tools, weapons, etc.) - predominantly made of bronze - true works of art can be found.

PAINTING

In general, Roman paintings originated from Pompeii and Herculaneum unfortunately were buried by the eruption of Mount Vesuvius. Roman painters simultaneously employed realism and imagination in their works.

Roman sculptures were characterized by more realistic traces

The oldest known Roman paintings are the frescoes discovered in a tomb on the Esquiline Hill, dating from the 3rd century BCE, approximately. Similar to sculpture, Roman painting, in its early phase, reflects Etruscan influence and later influences from Italic and Hellenic sources.

Thereby, These influences led to the development of four distinct styles. The first style, called incrustation, imitated works from Anatolia and the island of Delos, reproducing multicolored marble veneers. Between 70 BCE and 20 CE, the second architectural style featured improved techniques and was inspired by the Greek originals. They are panels that appear to open up into landscapes and palaces populated by characters from Greek mythology. The third style, the ornamental one, emerged in Pompeii in the late 1st century BCE. Realism gave way to idealization, and mythical characters entirely dominated the scenes. The fourth style corresponds to the reign of Nero, spanning the years 54 to 68 CE. Mosaics also played a significant role in Roman mural art, with strong Eastern influences.

MUSIC AND DANCE

It is known today that the musical culture from the eastern side of the Mediterranean, primarily from Greece, brought by the Roman legions, was altered and significantly simplified. Nonetheless, their musical and acoustic theories, instrument construction principles, repertoire of melodies and notation system formed the foundation of Western music in subsequent times.

In contrast, Roman dance did not follow the steps of Etruscan culture, unlike what happened in other forms of art. Apparently, Etruscan women played an important role in pair dances performed without masks in public places. Roman culture, steeped in its well-known rationalism, was quite averse to dance. Until the early 3rd century, such bodily movements were confined to procedural forms related to military and agricultural rituals.

Later, Etruscan and Greek influences spread, but those who danced were considered suspicious, effeminate, and even dangerous by the Roman aristocracy. Cicero, for example, emphasized that dance was a sign of madness. The Greek cult of Dionysus included inducing ecstasy through convulsive dance.

In the Roman Empire, dances were turned into festivals for Bacchus, initially exclusively for women and held for three days a year. Although secretive, these cults expanded, started to include men, and occurred as often as five times a month. In 186 BCE, on the grounds of obscenity, they were banned and their practitioners were subjected to relentless persecution, comparable only to the persecution of Christians. Their secretive society character posed a threat to the State. Around 150 BCE, the closure of all dance schools was ordered, but this did not eliminate the practice. Dancers and teachers were increasingly brought from other countries.

THEATER

This artistic representation was heavily based on Greek customs, even though there was already a rather incipient theatrical tradition in the Italian peninsula with Etruscan influence. In 240 BCE, it is believed that a translated Greek play was first presented during Roman games. The first Roman author to produce a more refined work was Cneius Naevius, who debuted in 235 BCE. The historical theater was his original initial creation. He even included in his plays - considered sharp and frank - critiques of the Roman aristocracy. He may have been imprisoned or exiled for this.

Therefore, the great poet Quintus Ennius, who succeeded Naevius, decided to adapt his talents to the demands of that context and dedicated himself to translating Greek tragedies. It was not until the late 2nd century BCE that true Latin comedy emerged.

Theatrical performances were part of the free entertainment offered during public festivals. However, from the very beginning, Roman theater depended on popular taste in a way that had never occurred in Greece. Thus, if a play did not please the audience, the festival organizer was required to return part of the funds received. Therefore, even during the republican time, there was a certain anxiety to offer the audience something that would please them.

Roman emperors shamelessly used this fact, providing "bread and circuses" - as the famous expression coined by the satirist Juvenal suggests - to distract the people from their miserable living conditions. The grand Colosseum and other amphitheaters throughout the empire attest to the power and grandeur of Rome, but not to its artistic energy.

There is no reason to believe that these constructions were intended for anything other than banal and degrading spectacles. The arenas were entirely occupied by gladiators in deadly combats, beasts goaded to pieces and Christians covered in pitch, used as human torches. It is no wonder that both writers and a different-minded audience began to view the theater as an unworthy and humiliating manifestation.

During the imperial period, the tragedies, for small private venues or for declamation without staging, emerged. Works by Seneca, a Stoic philosopher and principal advisor to Nero, belong to this category and exerted significant influence during the Renaissance, especially in England. Still during the Republic, mime and pantomime became the most popular theatrical forms. Based on actors' improvisations and physical agility, they provided ample opportunity for the audacious presentation of immoral and pornographic scenes. During the persecution of Christians under Nero and Domitian, the Christian faith was ridiculed. However, after the triumph of Christianity, theatrical performances were summarily banned.

ARTISTIC LEGACY

Despite the undeniable influence of Greek art, it is equally undeniable that the Roman artistic movement managed to form its own identity quite quickly. Through the realistic and extremely faithful representation of individuals - in contrast to Greece, which sought to idealize what was depicted -, the Romans presented, in their works, true figures of the social caste.

Furthermore, Rome was a clearly visual society. With the vast majority of its population being illiterate and even unable to speak the erudite Latin that circulated among the elite, visual arts served as a kind of literature accessible to the masses, confirming ideologies and disseminating the image of eminent personalities. In this context, sculpture enjoyed a privileged position, occupying all spaces - public and private - and populating cities with countless examples in various techniques.

Despite notable influences from past artistic movements, the Romans incorporated innovations in two main fields: portraiture and descriptive relief. The portrait itself, as an artistic process, went through various stages, as it not only closely reflected fashions but also manifested successively in significant moments, places and ultra-realistic trends, illustrating the most realistic as possible and later aiding in the execution of sculptures.

The historical theme of these narrative reliefs became Rome's most original contribution to this art form, always exalting military achievements, almost like a comic book. Another important form of expression was mosaics, which were later extensively used in the Middle Ages.

Given this context, it is possible to highlight that Roman art, in its context of conquests, contrary to what many people claim, was very valuable and left important legacies for future nations. With a more utilitarian character, the Romans brought the artistic environment into everyday life and brought reality to art works that had previously represented only an unattainable ideal.

11

A PEOPLE OF FAITH

FROM THE WORSHIP OF GREEK ORIGIN GODS TO THE TIMES OF CHRISTIANIZATION, ROMANS ALWAYS DEMONSTRATED A STRONG RELIGIOUS INCLINATION

The variety of Roman religion was quite pronounced and encompassed virtually all aspects of life. The truth is that the inhabitants of Ancient Rome worshiped various supernatural beings - from gods with roots in Greece to spirits capable of inhabiting natural elements such as storms, trees and rocks.

Thus, the ancient Romans were considered polytheistic, as they held a strong belief in different gods. These deities were anthropomorphic, meaning they had qualities and also flaws characteristic of humans, and they were represented in human form. The State promoted an official religion that paid homage to the great gods of Greek origin but with Latin names.

RELIGION AND STATE

The most important deity for the Romans was Jupiter. To the people, he was a powerful and very stern father and the ruler of all other gods. Juno, the queen of the gods, as she was Jupiter's sister and wife, and Minerva, the virgin goddess of wisdom and Jupiter's daughter, joined the supreme god to form the central triad in official public cults. Sacrifices, prayers, and rituals were sanctioned by the State. The three gods shared the Capitolium, the most famous and important temple in Rome, located in the central region of the city.

This place of worship was built in the 6th century BCE on the rocky Capitoline Hill and adorned with 24 stone columns, each over 65 feet high. Inside the temple, the religious people would find three inner chambers, with the statues of the gods in the main one. According to

View of the Capitolium, temple of worship of Jupiter, Juno and Minerva

historians, the internal layout of the Capitolium was quite similar to that of Etruscan temples.

Jupiter, Juno, and Minerva received offerings from the faithful, as these deities had the role of safeguarding the physical security and prosperity of Rome. To honor the first one - considered the best and greatest - the Romans held a festival of military and sports exercises in the Circus Maximus. During the imperial period, this competition venue could accommodate up to 250,000 people in stone and concrete seats to watch gladiator fights, chariot races, public executions and even enactments of hunts of wild animals imported from various parts of the world.

EXPENSIVE, BUT NECESSARY

Building the temple in the Capitolium was not cheap for the government's coffers, which at the time did not yet boast the financial power of the times to come. Even so, the expense was worth it, as the Romans believed that winning the goodwill of the gods was a real necessity for national defense against more aggressive neighbors.

At the same time, the inhabitants of Rome also believed that the gods ordered people to take responsibility for their own safety. Hence, the Romans in the 6th century BCE built a huge wall around the city as well.

Ten Commandments Tablets: relationship of Hebrews with their God contrasted with that of The Romans with their deities.

MORALITY

The Romans did not link the worship of deities with the need for acceptable moral behavior. For them, the gods were not the originators of the society's moral code. This belief contrasted significantly with that of the Hebrews, who had their conduct governed by God through the Ten Commandments and other laws divinely transmitted through the life of the prophet Moses.

In reality, the Roman gods seemed to show a great interest in how people treated them, but they had little concern for how individuals lived among themselves. Deceit in business, lying, or mutual aggression were not seen as actions subject to divine punishment, according to the Roman understanding. So, even though they believed that Jupiter could punish someone for breaking a sworn contract, the punishment would occur because the person offended the god by disregarding the commitment made under his witness.

The Roman historian Cicero summarized Roman beliefs as follows: "Jupiter is called 'the best' and 'the greatest' not because he makes us just, moderate or wise, but because he makes us secure, wealthy, and well-provided". Over the centuries, Romans maintained this understanding of the divine nature.

However, the people of Rome believed that some of their most important values - such as loyalty - were special divine beings or forces. This is evident from the fact that in 181 BCE, the Romans built a temple to Pietas, a type of personification of the central value related to respect for the gods and moral obligations. In the temple, there was a statue of a goddess representing these qualities.

PRIESTHOOD

In the Republican era, the class of priests who led the official cults of the various Roman gods consisted of both men and women from the highest social hierarchy. These individuals did not consider priesthood as a professional career but rather as a fulfillment of one aspect of a successful public life in the city of Rome.

Their primary function was to ensure the goodwill of the gods toward the nation and the State. This relationship was referred to as the "peace of the gods". In order to attain the favor of the deities, priests and priestesses were often called upon to conduct festivals, sacrifices and other rituals in strict accordance with the traditions of their ancestors.

Nothing could be done differently. If the ancient prayer formulas were spoken incorrectly or if there was even a single mistake in a word, the entire procedure had to be restarted. Thus, as Rome became the home to numerous shrines and temples over time, these sacred activities consumed a great deal of time and effort. Moreover, the associated costs were quite high.

Besides, official State events always had a preparatory religious ritual. For example, Senate meetings usually began with the analysis of religious matters deemed most relevant to the state. Military commanders also performed divination rites to discern the will of the gods. So, the gods could assist them in understanding the best time to undertake their campaigns.

The most important council of priests, which had 15 members during the Republic, was responsible for advising magistrates on their religious responsibilities as agents of the State. The leader of this group was Pontifex Maximus, who held the highest position in the Roman public religion. He had the greatest authority over religious matters that directly affected local governance. The political significance of the Pontifex Maximus led influential men to seek this position, which, in the 3rd century BCE, was filled through elections.

FESTIVALS

In the beginning, most Roman religious events were rooted in the aspirations of the agricultural community. Traditionally, the religion of Rome sought protection for its crops, the primary means of survival for the early community. Thereby, prayers often focused on asking the gods for help in achieving bountiful harvests, preventing diseases and ensuring healthy reproduction among domesticated animals.

The massive sanctuary in Praeneste – modern-day Palestrina, a city 20 miles from Rome – was the place where people sought divine assistance to ensure food. This five-level structure was one of the largest religious buildings in all of ancient Italy.

In general, religious rituals did not change significantly over the years. This was because, according to Roman thinking, the addition of anything new to the customary homage to the gods could offend them and provoke undesirable divine wrath upon humans.

Therefore, the religion of the Late Republic retained many ancient rituals. One of them was the festival of Saturnalia, held in December, during which the social order was temporarily inverted. According to the playwright and scholar Accius (170 BCE to 80 BCE), during this festival, people feasted in both rural and urban areas and "every master played the part of a servant to his slaves". On the one hand, this reversal of roles served to release tensions caused by the inequalities between these two groups. On the other hand, it aimed to reinforce the sense of obligation of the servants to their masters by symbolizing the kindness that should be repaid with loyal service.

As devout polytheists, inhabitants of Ancient Rome believed that there could be gods who demanded veneration but had not yet accepted it. In cases of national emergencies, the State would often seek divine protection against foreign deities that did not have a customary cult among the Romans. One example was the importation of the cult of Asclepius, the Greek god of medicine, in 293 BCE, intending to rid Rome of a severe plague. Other citizens imported the cult of the Greek god Dionysus – better known as Bacchus among the Romans. However, this veneration of Bacchus generated some discontent because it involved morally questionable sexual

City of Palestrina, in Italy, place which housed a big sanctuary where people prayed to get food

rites. Nevertheless, the government did not show much interest in these controversies unless they posed a threat to the State, as would happen in later years with the rise of Christianity.

FAMILY

Within the family, religious elements were very present in Roman homes. Every Roman household had spaces considered sacred. The statue of Juno – who had two faces – was placed at the entrance of the house. One face looked towards the street and the other faced into the home. In this way, it was believed that this deity ensured protection for the home, preventing the entry of enemies.

Families also maintained a shrine in the form of a cabinet to hold figurines representing benevolent spirits, such as the spirit of provisions and ancestors. The residents of the house also hung masks of illustrious dead ancestors on the walls of the living room. It was a way to remind the new generation of the importance of living up to ancient and virtuous ideals. Indeed, the primary source of Roman morality was directly linked to the strong sense of family tradition present in these practices and instilled by the parents. What helped prevent immoral behavior the most was the fear of losing respect, not the fear of divine punishment.

Household rituals were so common that they complemented even more mundane activities, such as breastfeeding a child and fertilizing the soil for planting. The performance of these small religious events was linked to the respectful reverence that Romans sought to have and the quest for security in a world full of dangers.

The willingness of the gods to intervene in basically all aspects of daily life made the relationship between humans and the divine quite complex. This was because the Romans did not believe that the gods tended to love humans. Thus, the deities could punish any creature without even having a plausible reason.

This relationship was even more challenging because there was no clear communication between the two parties. Therefore, people did everything in their power to discover the divine will. This constant obligation to understand the gods' desires motivated religious activity in Rome.

PERSECUTION OF CHRISTIANS

During the imperial period, amid polytheism, the Roman government displayed deep concern over the increasing number of Christians.

Followers of a man named Jesus refused to participate in the religious ceremonies regularly conducted in Rome. That was the main reason for the persecution of this group, considered a sect of Judaism.

Furthermore, Christian gatherings aroused suspicion. Thereby, they were accused of engaging in acts considered immoral and criminal. These men often met before sunrise or at night, frequently in caves. Among the accusations against them were cannibalism, incest and even infanticide as a form of worship to their deity. Even the practice of greeting one another with a kiss was deemed as an immoral behavior.

The Christians of that time also refused to worship the emperor as a god. For the Romans, bowing before the ruler was a demonstration of loyalty. Throughout the Empire, numerous statues were placed in public spaces for reverence. Followers of the new religion did not engage in such worship because it was reserved solely for Jesus, their true king. This stance marked them as threatening revolutionaries in the eyes of Rome.

The first State-sponsored persecution of Christians took place during the reign of Emperor Claudius, between 41 and 54 CE, when he ordered the expulsion of Jews from Rome due to their disputes concerning a certain Christ. In general, Romans viewed Christianity as a collection of irrational practices that sinister magicians and wizards used to deceive ignorant people.

UNFOUNDED ACCUSATIONS

The flames that consumed a significant part of Rome in the year 65 were blamed by Emperor Nero on the Christians. This was Nero's way of diverting attention away from himself, as the people held him responsible for the fire.

Nero then began a three-year persecution of Jesus's followers. Some historians suggest that the apostles Peter and Paul were among those killed in the hunt.

The historian Cornelius Tacitus (54 to 120 CE), even though he was a harsh critic of Christians, accused Nero of unjustly blaming the religious group. Nevertheless, he expressed his conviction that the Christians deserved the most severe punishments because their superstitions led them to commit abominations.

Therefore, Christians were regarded as despicable people capable of horrendous crimes, such as infanticide – the Romans believed that during the Lord's Supper when partaking of the Eucharist, the Christians sacrificed a child and consumed its flesh – and incest – this was their interpretation of the exchange of the peace that occurred during the Eucharistic celebration between "brothers and sisters". These accusations were fueled by rumors among the general populace and were sanctioned by the authority of the emperor, who persecuted and condemned Christians to death.

MORE PERSECUTIONS

Marcus Aurelius (161-180) was considered a philosopher and educated emperor. In his frequent writings, the king showed great disdain for Christianity. He said that this religion was madness because it proposed to the "common and ignorant people a way of behaving that only philosophers like him could understand and practice after long meditations and disciplines". According to Marcus Aurelius, the common population was not capable of practicing things like universal brotherhood, forgiveness and sacrifice for others without expecting a reward.

Hence, the emperor directly attacked Christianity in the second century. He decided to prohibit any practice of this religion, as he believed it posed a danger to the State. The situation of the Christians, which was already complicated, became even more difficult.

Various communities in Asia Minor, founded by the apostle Paul, were constantly robbed and plundered. In Rome, the philosopher Justin and a group of Jesus's followers were sentenced to death.

Intellectuals opposed to Christianity, like Marcus Aurelius, Galen (129-200) and Celsus, countered the doctrine. For them, philosophy was the only path to human salvation: "The 'salvation' from the disorder of events, annihilation of death and pain can only be found in 'philosophical wisdom' on the part of an elite of rare intellectuals. It is madness for Christians to place this 'salvation' in 'faith' in a crucified man (like slaves) in Palestine (a marginal province) who was declared resurrected. Christians must be eliminated as transgressors of human civilization".

Later, in the third century, there were years of terrible persecution of Christians. The hunt for Christianity was revived in the name of ethnic cleansing. As the Roman Empire was undergoing a profound economic and social crisis, the rulers saw that the only way to save the nation was to return to a homogenous line of thinking. Thus, the followers of Jesus were to be annihilated.

However, the systematic persecutions proved to be ineffective. This was because the Christians themselves despised honors and many aimed to die for their religious cause. Furthermore, the doctrine widely spread by them had won the minds of many people who had been disregarded by the Empire for years.

CHRISTIAN EMPIRE

The movement of persecution against Christians only came to a definitive end in 321 CE, following the Edict of Constantine I, which guaranteed freedom of worship in the Roman Empire. However, the story surrounding the end of the persecution of Jesus's followers began a few years earlier.

Starting from the year 306, with the failure of the tetrarchy system – the State divided into four parts – there was significant confusion in the distribution of power in Rome. In the Western part, the elimination of Maximian and Galerius left only Constantine in prominence, who was proclaimed "augustus". Maxentius, Maximian's son, also received the designation of "augustus".

Maxentius resided in Rome, while Constantine, who had formed an alliance with Licinius, the Eastern emperor, was in Gaul. In the year 312, Constantine used the alleged mistreatment inflicted by Maxentius on his subjects as a pretext to lead a major expedition to liberate Italy.

Constantine's action was bold, as he had only 25,000 men, while his opponent had about 100,000 soldiers. His army quickly crossed the Alps, surpassing the Montgenèvre Pass. Hence, he seized the city of Susa, setting it ablaze, which opened the way to Turin. The most violent battle took place in this location. The army of Maxentius's generals had a significant advantage with their formidable warriors clad in iron armor and mounted on horses. However, Constantine used a tactic that disrupted the enemy army and achieved an important triumph. The victory helped him enter Milan majestically. Further victories led Constantine's men to march to Rome.

Maxentius, who was very superstitious, had allegedly been tormented by nightmares and bad omens that prevented him from advancing against his rival. Influenced by the wizard of his court, he decided to confront his adversary north of the city of Rome.

On October 28, 312, Constantine took the initiative in the battle. His attack quickly disorganized Maxentius's army. Some of his men threw themselves into the Tiber River, while others sought refuge on a bridge that, unable to support their weight, collapsed. The soldiers were swept away by the current, and Maxentius himself drowned.

Following the complete triumph, Constantine was welcomed in Rome as a true liberator. His soldiers, who found Maxentius's corpse, followed the victor's procession, carrying the head of the deceased emperor stuck on a spear, amid the applause of the Roman citizens. With this victory, Constantine came to dominate the Roman Empire on his own.

Subsequently, in the year 313, Emperor Constantine converted to Christianity and allowed the cult of this religion throughout the Empire. Almost eight decades later, the tables would turn completely. In 391, not only did Christianity become the official religion of Rome, but all the other pagan sects were persecuted. It was from this moment onwards that the Christian Church began to gain more strength and was transformed into a powerful institution.

The patriarchs of Christianity spread throughout the region controlled by the Romans. The patriarchates were divided among the cities of Alexandria, Jerusalem, Antioch, Constantinople and Rome. By the emperor's order in 455, the patriarch of Rome became, from this moment on, the highest authority of the church, under the designation now known as the Pope.

In the year 325, Emperor Constantine promoted a meeting in Nicaea with ecclesiastical authorities to define the main beliefs that should govern the conduct of Christians. This agreement was called the Council of Nicaea and became a milestone in the constitution of the religion. Other meetings were held in the future to align the church doctrinally.

MARTYRS

Condemned Christians, according to historian Tacitus, were killed torn apart by dogs, crucified or even burned alive with torches which were used to illuminate the darkness when night came. During Nero's government, the emperor offered his gardens to watch this "spectacle".

Tacitus himself states in his writings that, over time, a certain sense of pity for Christians grew, as they were "sacrificed not due to common interest, but to the cruelty of the prince".

12

THE DECLINE OF THE EMPIRE

FROM THE 3RD CENTURY ONWARDS, SUCCESSIVE FOREIGN INVASIONS AND THE RECURRING AND IRRESPONSIBLE SPENDING ON THE ARMY HELPED TO LEAD THE POWER TO ITS COLLAPSE

Living became much more difficult for most of the inhabitants of the Roman Empire from the 3rd century CE onwards due to a combination of various disasters that created a crisis in both the government and society. This scenario, unimaginable a few years earlier, marked the beginning of the decline of the great power of that time.

Frequent invasions by foreigners along the northern and eastern borders for several years forced the Roman emperors to significantly increase the size of the army. However, the expansion of defense forces adversely affected the imperial finances because the process of large territorial conquests - which had provided substantial rewards through plunder - had ceased. By that time, the army was incurring only expenses.

To make matters worse, the so-called non-military economy expanded much less than needed to offset these expenses. In other words, expenses grew much more than revenues and the fiscal deficit in the Empire became almost inevitable.

This uncomfortable situation led to a profound crisis in national defense. Desperate emperors seeking higher revenues damaged the Roman economy and eroded people's confidence in security. This environment encouraged ambitious generals to seize power through their personal armies, leading to yet another civil war that lasted for decades and completely destabilized the imperial government.

Detail on Arch of Constantine, in Rome, illustrates battle between Roman legion and Barbarians

INVADERS

Deeply concerned about national sovereignty, the leaders of Rome had been conducting campaigns to combat invaders since the 1st century CE, during the reign of Domitian. The Germans were considered the most aggressive invaders. They were disorganized groups from the north who often crossed the Danube and Rhine rivers to raid the provinces in that region.

These groups began launching attacks that resulted in significant losses during the rule of Antoninus Pius (138 to 161 CE) and intensified their incursions during the reign of Marcus Aurelius (161 to 180 CE). Battles against the Roman army became more frequent, allowing the Germans to become better organized militarily over time.

As a strategy to mitigate the damage, Rome used the enemy's weapon to its advantage. Emperors started to hire Germanic fighters as auxiliary soldiers and positioned them precisely on the frontiers to halt the advance of more invading groups. Recruiting foreigners became one of the main short-term alternatives for national defense. Nevertheless, the side effect was that it allowed the Germans to gain knowledge of the comfortable Roman way of life. This increased the tendency of these barbarians to want to stay in the territory of the Empire permanently. It is important to note that this movement was a precursor to the territorial boundaries of modern-day Europe.

SPENDINGS

Around the year 200 CE, the Roman army experienced a significant increase in size. During this period, historians estimate that there were

100,000 more troops than in the time of Augustus. It is believed that recruitment in the early 3rd century reached nearly 400,000 men.

However, to keep this large contingent satisfied, it was important to provide regular pay since the career was quite challenging. Additionally, a vast amount of supplies was required for this sizable force. In a temporary fort in a particular frontier area, archaeologists found approximately one million iron nails, equivalent to 22,000 pounds of the material. Such a camp also needed 17 miles of boards for fortifications. Finally, it is estimated that equipping a legion of 5 to 6 thousand men required the leather from 54,000 calves.

Besides this big demand for resources, the inflation during this period caused the prices of such commodities to rise significantly. The primary reason for the price increase is believed to be the "Roman Peace" period, which increased the demand for products and services in the local economy.

Over time, some Roman emperors responded to inflated prices by tampering with the silver coins issued in the ruler's name, the most important form of official currency. Coinage adulteration was done by using less silver in the coin without decreasing its nominal value. Thus, the government could buy more while spending less.

However, merchants were astute and were not easily deceived. They raised prices even further to compensate for the losses caused by the tampered coins, which led to hyperinflation. By the end of the 2nd century CE, this turbulent situation resulted in a permanent trade deficit in the Roman Empire. Nevertheless, the soldiers continued to demand good pay and the situation eventually led to a profound financial crisis in the government.

WORSENING

Septimius Severus (145-211) and his sons Caracalla and Geta were responsible for ensuring the realization of the economic ruin. They drained the public coffers to satisfy the desires of the army. Additionally, the trio was known for their unorthodox spending from the treasury, which further destabilized the already ailing Empire.

Highly experienced in the military, Severus began to vie for the position of emperor after the assassination of Commodus – Marcus Aurelius' son – which caused a major crisis in Roman territory. He had to defeat his main contenders for the throne in a violent civil war to assume power in the year 193.

In pursuit of financial resources for the army and glory for his family, the emperor vigorously pursued the dream of conquering new territories by launching campaigns beyond the eastern and western borders of the Empire, in Mesopotamia and Scotland. However, the expeditions did not yield the expected profits, and he failed in his attempt to fix the budget deficit.

On the other hand, the soldiers became increasingly concerned since inflation eroded the purchasing power of their salaries to almost nothing, particularly with the deductions resulting from the costs of basic supplies and clothing from their pay, according to the ancient army regulations. Thus, the troops awaited monetary compensation (a sort of bonus) from the emperor to offset their losses.

Severus not only disbursed staggering sums to provide the money but also decided to improve the soldiers' long-term conditions by raising the regular pay rate by a third. The considerable size of the Roman army at that time made this pay increase much higher than the national treasury could bear. Consequently, inflation grew even further.

Even in the face of an economic calamity, the Emperor showed little concern for the serious consequences. It is true that on his deathbed, he allegedly told his children: "Maintain good relations between you, enrich the soldiers and pay no attention to anyone else".

The problem was that his children only followed part of his advice. Caracalla did not seem so keen on maintaining a good relationship with Geta and instead murdered him to secure control of the government for himself. His reign, known for its violence and debauchery, effectively marked the end of the peace and prosperity of the Imperial Golden Age.

Caracalla increased the pay of the soldiers by almost 50 percent. Furthermore, he squandered plenty of money on colossal construction projects, the largest of which was a sequence of public toilets that extended over countless city blocks in the capital.

The emperor's extravagance in spending placed unsustainable pressure on public officials in the provinces for tax collection and, of cour-

Ruins of the public toilets built throughout Caracalla

se, on the citizens who were compelled to pay exorbitant taxes. Caracalla managed to devastate any possibility of economic recovery for Rome. The unfavorable environment provided the perfect excuse for the emperor's bodyguard to assassinate him in the year 217 and seize the throne.

DISORDER

After the Severan emperors, a succession of problems took over the Roman Empire and reached its peak crisis point in the 3rd century. Initially, political instability was the most immediate effect of the economic crisis. For a period of nearly 70 years, a large number of emperors and claimants to the throne fiercely fought for power. Approximately 30 men assumed the government or simply claimed it. Some "emperors" even held power simultaneously. The situation was akin to anarchy.

The 3rd century was filled with civil wars which severely harmed the people and the economy. Lack of security reached its highest point. Hyperinflation continued and life became a lamentation in much of the powerful Empire. Agriculture suffered, as farmers could not maintain their usual production due to the ongoing warfare. In this period, warring armies damaged a significant portion of the crops in search of food.

Members of city councils faced increasingly higher tax collection due to demands of the emperors, who rapidly alternated in power. The complete administrative disorder led local elites to stop supporting their communities.

Adding to the internal issues, more foreign enemies took advantage of Roman weakness to launch attacks. The situation became critical when the king of the Sassanid Persian Empire, Shapur I, captured Valerian – ruler from 253 to 260 – in Syria, in 260.

Even the experienced Emperor Aurelian – in power between 270 and 275 – succumbed to the chaotic situation and could only focus on immediate defense operations, such as Egypt and Asia Minor's recovery from Zenobia, the warrior queen of Palmyra in Syria. He also surrounded Rome with a 10-mile-long wall to protect the city from surprise attacks, especially by the Germanic tribes, which were already approaching from the north. Parts of this construction, such as its towers and gates, can still be seen in various locations in the Italian capital today.

EARTHQUAKES, DISEASES AND COLLAPSE

Amid the Roman administrative failures, natural disasters struck. Earthquakes ravaged buildings and virulent epidemics swept through the entire Mediterranean region. To make matters worse, the reliability of food sources became less certain, leaving the population weaker and more susceptible. Civil wars decimated both soldiers and civilians.

The collapsed scenario made the border areas very inviting for foreign attacks. Wandering bands of thieves also appeared within the Empire as economic conditions worsened.

Adherents of the traditional polytheistic religion began to believe that the gods were against them. The reason? They believed that the deities had become angry because of the Christians, who refused to worship the Roman gods. The already highly conflict-ridden atmosphere became even more inhospitable with the intensified persecution of Jesus's followers. Emperor Decius (who ruled between 249 and 251) led violent attacks against the Christians with the clear goal of eliminating the group.

Emperor Gallienus (reigning from 260 to 268) restored religious peace and ended the persecution. Nevertheless, by the 280s, there was no denying that the Roman Empire was on the brink of collapse.

REDEMPTION

Diocletian could be considered an unlikely hero by the Romans of the late 3rd century. The young man from the rugged region of Dalmatia in the Balkans began his military career with little education. However, his courage and intelligence propelled him up the ranks and, with the support of the army, he was declared emperor in 284.

He managed to end the crisis of the 3rd century through an autocratic government, that is, based on his own ideas. With the military's support, he was formally recognized as dominus (master) instead of "first man". The governmental system instituted by Diocletian came to be known as the Dominate, which meant the absolute power of the emperor. This eliminated any possibility of shared authority between the ruler and the Roman elite. The positions of senator, consul and other roles inherent to the Republic were maintained but only as a façade.

A characteristic of this new mode of governance was the selection of officials from the lower strata of society, based on competence and loyalty to the ruler. Thus, the tradition of appointing administrators from the upper class was discontinued.

Furthermore, the rulers of the Dominate abandoned the tradition initiated by Augustus of wearing simple and everyday clothing. They began to don garments adorned with jewels and dazzling crowns. As a way to highlight the distinction between the "master" and common people, in the palace, various veils separated waiting rooms from the inner space where the ruler conducted his audiences.

In this period, a theological structure was developed to legitimize the government. For example, Diocletian adopted the title Jovius, proclaiming himself to be a descendant of Jupiter (the main Roman god).

The words of the emperor took on a more aggressive tone. The emperors of the Dominate reaffirmed autocracy in the punishment of crimes and in the realm of law. Their orders carried the force of law and the assemblies of the Republic no longer operated as sources of legislation.

NEW TETRARCHY

Even with his success as a ruler, Diocletian believed that the Roman Empire was too vast to be defended and administered from a single center. Thereby, he concluded that dividing the government into two parts would be the best solution. Through a bold process, he separated the territory into East and West. In practice, he created an Eastern Roman Empire and a Western Roman Empire, although this division was not formally recognized.

After the first stage of administrative reform, Diocletian made two more subdivisions - one in each region - and appointed trusted men for a kind of cooperative government. Each one controlled a district, its respective capital, and the military forces. To prevent any disagreements or disunity, the highest-ranking leader - in this specific case, Diocletian - acted as the emperor and should receive the loyalty of the other co-emperors.

The new tetrarchy aimed to cease the isolation of the imperial government in Rome, which was far from the vast borders of the great Empire and the issues that arose in these more distant regions.

These decisions were historic as the creation of the four regions made Rome no longer the capital of the Romans after a thousand years. The new capitals were chosen taking into consideration their utility as military command posts: Milan, in the northern region of Italy; Sirmium, near the Danube River border; Trier, on the Rhine River border and Nicomedia, in Asia Minor.

As a result, Italy became just another section of the Empire, on equal terms with the other provinces and subject to the same taxation system.

ECONOMIC REFORM

The emperor also took every possible step to restore the economic power of Rome. Initially, Diocletian sought to restore the importance of silver and gold coins by reducing the amount of gold content in the coins while keeping their nominal value. Additionally, he introduced bronze fractional coins with a thin silver coating for everyday transactions to facilitate change. These coins, however, were depreciated, and many merchants began to refuse them as payment forms.

At this time, mints needed to be expanded to meet the trade's needs, public works construction and the increased number of military and civilians.

The ruler also imposed tax reforms to levy different taxes based on social classes. For this reason, he conducted a census of the population every five years and, based on the data collected about their assets, taxed citizens. These taxes were often paid in kind. For example, farmers paid in grains, wines, oils and meats. Cash payments, on the other hand, were made by merchants and artisans in the cities.

Challenges in agriculture needed to be addressed promptly, as this sector was considered the foundation of manufacturing, where raw materials were extracted from nature. Diocletian's measure was ruralization, which involved leasing land to peasants, farmers and tenants, who had to pay a tax on annual agricultural production.

Adequate developments in agriculture, trade, livestock and craftsmanship were ensured when various peaceful Germanic people were added as farmers or soldiers to defend the Roman border.

As for the common people in large urban centers, they were given political representation reflecting the new economic reality. According to this measure, they were required to continue in their respective professions and pass them down to their descendants. They also needed to form or join a kind of cooperative that brought together workers in the same line of work.

In the year 301, Diocletian began combating hyperinflation by issuing the Edict on Maximum Prices, which set limits on wage earnings for working hours and price ceilings for consumer products. In Sicily, the State was required to regulate the production of cereals and the exchange of goods, preventing farmers from selling their crops to the so-called middlemen. Hence, official buyers from Rome were responsible for controlling planting, inspecting the harvest and monopolizing transportation, focusing on the quality of production and trade.

Diocletian's government also became known for creating numerous job opportunities through investments in constructions, expansion or renovation of viaducts, bridges, roads, triumphal arches, imperial buildings, aqueducts, public works, theaters for theatrical performances, domes, among other architectural projects.

To reduce the costs of these interventions, concrete, a cheaper material, was used alongside bricks. In simpler houses, tiles, pebbles and stucco were also used.

Diocletian introduced public baths as a form of leisure, which could gather up to 3,000 people. The citizens of Rome would meet at these places to talk in centrally air-conditioned halls. They were not just places where people simply bathed, but they also featured bars, restaurants, barbershops, bookstores, brothels, massage parlors, clothing stores, spaces for sports, pools, areas for physical exercise and heated rooms. It was a form of entrepreneurship to drive the Roman economy more vigorously.

Despite the success of his rule, Diocletian decided to abdicate the government of the Empire. On the first of March in 305, he announced his decision to step down from the throne during a ceremony in the region of Nicomedia. He withdrew to Dalmatia with a sense of fulfilled duty.

CONSTANTINE

Diocletian's administrative accomplishments are undeniable. However, the emperor went to great lengths to have absolute control over the government. In the year 303, he initiated a severe persecution of Christians in the Empire, destroying their churches, ordering the burning of their sacred texts and killing those who refused to participate in official religious rites. In reality, his interest was not religious, but rather to maintain order during a period known as the Great Persecution.

Constantine, who succeeded his predecessor in 306, changed the religious - and consequently, the political - history of the Empire by converting to Christianity. It was the first time that a ruler of Rome proclaimed his alliance with the Christian religion. Constantine adopted Christianity for the same reason that Diocletian had persecuted it: he believed he was securing divine protection for the Empire and himself.

The emperor did not make his new personal faith the official religion but decreed religious tolerance. The reality is that he did not want to incur the wrath of polytheism adherents, as they were still far more numerous than the Christians.

Nevertheless, he made significant efforts to promote Christianity by constructing the Basilica of Saint John Lateran to serve as the cathedral of the Bishop of Rome. He also built another enormous basilica dedicated to Saint Peter. This building, completed in 349 CE, after decades of construction, served as a center of worship for over a thousand years. In the 16th century, it was demolished to make way for the current structure.

Constantine also returned all the properties confiscated by Diocletian to the Christians. However, to avoid problems with non-Christians who had acquired the lands at auctions, he ordered financial compensation for their losses.

But his rule was not solely marked by benevolence toward Christians. He also invested in the construction of a new capital between 324 and 330. The emperor founded Constantinople in the place of ancient Byzantium (now Istanbul, Turkey) at the mouth of the Black Sea. In this new project, Constantine decided to place statues of the customary gods of the city to avoid causing discord with tradition. With this behavior, he aimed to maintain good relations and prevent unnecessary political implications for his government, which had been proceeding quite smoothly during all these years. Respecting Roman customs was one of his main principles.

Slowly, through religious syncretism, Christianity gained ground and

Image showing ruins of the ancient Palace of Diocletian:
Emperor restored the empire at the end of the 3rd century

became the official religion of the Roman Empire in 391, during the reign of Theodosius.

DIVISION OF EMPIRE

The plan of a tetrarchic government, instituted by Diocletian, did not hold. Nonetheless, the principle of dividing the administration bore fruit. Constantine waged an intense civil war at the beginning of his reign to achieve a unified government and abolished the tetrarchy due to concerns about disloyal leadership.

Towards the end of his reign, he was still hesitant to admit that the Empire needed more rulers. Nevertheless, Constantine designated his three sons as joint successors. However, rivalry among the brothers completely undermined any possibility of maintaining unity. By the end of the 4th century, the Empire was formally divided into two sections (Western and Eastern), each with its own emperor.

Time and disagreements led to a growing rift between the two halves. Constantinople was the capital of the Eastern Empire and held important qualities: it was situated on a fortified peninsula and was strategically located on trade routes. Additionally, Constantine had equipped the city with a forum, an imperial palace and a hippodrome for chariot races.

Geography also determined the location of the capital of the Western Empire. In 404, Emperor Honorius made Ravenna – a port on the northeast coast of Italy – the permanent capital of the West. It was protected by strong walls against land attacks, and its access to the sea prevented it from being entirely cut off from supplies in a possible siege. Nevertheless, as historian Thomas R. Martin noted, Ravenna never matched the size or splendor of Constantinople.

Meanwhile, the city of Rome had fallen into a sad decline that would, over the years, reduce it to the condition of an impoverished village, which had once been home to many Romans. The pompous locality entered a process of ruin.

BARBARIAN MIGRATIONS

The barbarians earned this name due to the impression the Romans had of the inhabitants from the north. Their different language, clothing and customs made them appear savage in the eyes of the

The various Germanic barbarians, in the 4th century A.D, who formed an ethnically diverse group, first migrated to Roman lands as refugees searching for another place fleeing the relentless attacks of the Huns. They sought safety and comfort provided by the Roman Empire. However, by the end of the 4th century CE, the influx of barbarians became much more substantial. These people were driven from the land which is now Eastern Europe, north of the Danube River.

The barbarians had little expectation of forming a unified nation as they were not politically or militarily united and they lacked a shared sense of identity. The only common thread among many of them was the Germanic origin of their languages.

The first group of Germanic barbarians to escape across the Roman border became known as the Visigoths. Dispersed due to the Hunnic attacks, they implored the Eastern Roman Emperor Valens, in 376, to allow them to migrate to the Balkans. The Visigoths were granted permission under the condition that their warriors would enlist in the Roman army to help defend against the Huns.

Nonetheless, some corrupt Roman officials, responsible for assisting the refugees, ended up exploiting the barbarians for profit, leading to their starvation. These officials even forced some of the Germans to sell their own people as slaves in exchange for dogs to eat.

Given this scenario, the Visigoths revolted. In 378, they defeated and killed Valens in Adrianople (modern-day European Turkey) and decimated two-thirds of the Roman forces. Valens's successor, Theodosius I (ruler between 379 and 395), had to renegotiate with the Visigoths, who were granted the right to stay permanently in the Empire, freedom to establish their own kingdom under their own laws and annual payments from the treasury.

Unable to fulfill this agreement, Western rulers began to force the barbarians into the Eastern Empire. They cut subsidies to the refugees and threatened total war if they did not leave.

Once again, the Visigoths responded. In 410, the barbarians captured Rome and terrorized the local population. When Alaric, the Visigothic commander, demanded gold, silver, movable goods and slaves from the city, the Romans reportedly asked, "What will be left for us?" To which the barbarian general is said to have replied, "Your lives".

Facing the grave situation, in 418, the Western Roman government agreed to settle them in southwest Gaul (modern-day France). There, they organized a State and became a slightly democratic tribal society. However, the problem for the Western Empire was just beginning. Concessions made to the Visigoths encouraged other barbarian groups to use force to conquer Roman territory. In 406, a group known as the Vandals, also fleeing from the Huns, crossed the Rhine River. This large group made its way through Gaul to the Spanish coast. In 429, 80,000 Vandals sailed to North Africa, where they captured the Roman province. Once there, they seized lands and imposed tribute payments. This happening further weakened the Western Empire.

In 455, they looted Rome and destroyed the central symbol of the old Empire's glory. The Vandals also disrupted the plans of the Eastern Empire when they broke the Mediterranean trade agreement, especially food supply.

In addition, numerous smaller groups took advantage of the total disorder caused by the more prominent bands to seize parts of the Western Empire. Among them were the Anglo-Saxons. This group, composed of Angles from Denmark and Saxons from northwest Germany, invaded Britain in the 440s CE after the Roman army was called to defend Italy against the Visigoths. The Anglo-Saxons established rule in Britain by wresting territory from the indigenous Celtic peoples and remaining Roman inhabitants. At the end of the 5th century, it was the turn of the Ostrogoths, coming from the east, to establish their rule in Italy.

END OF THE WESTERN EMPIRE

Several commanders of the Germanic army were called upon to assist in the defense of the central Roman region. However, in the 5th century, some of these generals took advantage of the power struggles among the Romans, vying for the position of emperor, and became mediators with political influence in deciding who would be the ruler at the time. Besides, The Germans could also depose the emperor, reducing the Roman emperor to a mere puppet in their hands.

The last man to occupy the throne under these conditions was a young boy named Romulus Augustulus. In the year 476, the barbarian commander Odoacer deposed him but showed mercy due to the young age of the boy, providing him with a pension to live in exile near Naples. The Germanic general proclaimed himself an independent king and brought an end to five centuries of Roman ethnic emperors. It marked the political end of the Western Roman Empire.

Nevertheless, Odoacer made an effort to maintain the Senate of Rome and even the consuls to show certain respect for tradition. Moreover, he sent envoys to Constantinople to demonstrate recognition to the Eastern Emperor and secure diplomatic support.

However, Constantinople was suspicious of this move and decided to hire the king of the Ostrogoths, Theodoric the Great, to eliminate Odoacer. He carried out the task, assassinated the intruder, but betrayed the Eastern Emperor. Theodoric established his own Germanic kingdom in Italian territory and kept the West under the rule of the Ostrogoths until the end of his life in the year 526.

In line with Odoacer's thinking, Theodoric desired to enjoy the more luxurious life of the imperial elite. He also aimed to maintain the traditions of the Roman Empire to ensure status for his new government. Once again, the Senate and the position of consul remained intact. As an Arian Christian, Theodoric followed the example set by Constantine and adopted a religious tolerance policy.

MELTING POT

The rise of the barbarians to the Western Throne, highlighted by historians as a significant political transformation in Europe during that time, resulted in profound sociocultural changes. The newly arrived inhabitants helped create new ways of life based on a fusion of traditions from different regions.

The Visigothic king Ataulfo, who ruled between 410 and 415, was an example of this. He married a Roman noblewoman and openly spoke about the integration of diverse customs: "At first, I wanted to erase the name of the Romans and turn their land into a Gothic empire, making to myself what Augustus had done. But I learned that the unbridled savagery of the Goths would never accept the rule of law, and that a State without law is not a State. Therefore, I chose a wiser path to glory: to renew the Roman name with Gothic vigor. I pray that future generations will remember me as the founder of a Roman restoration".

However, the Visigoths did not seem prepared to govern the Empire due to the old traditions they brought from northeastern Europe. In that region, they lived in small settlements whose economies relied on small-scale farming, herding and ironwork.

Free warrior assemblies were the only traditional form of political organization for the barbarians. The roles of leaders were largely limited to religious and military duties. Tribes and clans often experienced internal conflicts and violent hostilities. As a result, the Germanic kingdoms never matched the organizational structure of the ancient Roman government during the Golden Age of the Empire.

EASTERN EMPIRE

On the other side, the members of the Eastern Roman Empire sought to avoid the changes that had completely altered the Western half. Economic integrity and political unity were their hallmarks in the following centuries. Most of the time, contemporary historians refer to the Eastern Empire as the Byzantine Empire, a term derived from Byzantium, the former name of the capital.

The emperors in Constantinople used a combination of force, diplomacy and cunning bribes to repel migrations and send them westward (away from their territories). They also countered the aggression of the Sassanid Empire in Persia to the East and protected the East-West spice trade route. Thus, the rulers of the East largely preserved ancient traditions and the population of the region.

The last Eastern emperor to attempt to resurrect the old Roman Empire was Justinian (between 482 and 565). He launched Roman expeditions to try to suppress the Germanic peoples in the West, but such campaigns only served to fuel a distant dream and deplete the public coffers.

From the 7th century onward, the emperors lost vast territories to the violent onslaughts of Islamic armies, but they still managed to maintain the government in the capital for another 850 years.

13

THE ROMAN HERITAGE

THE DOMINION FADED AWAY OVER THE YEARS, BUT THE INFLUENCE OF THE ANCIENT POWER EXTENDED OVER THE CENTURIES THROUGH LAW, LANGUAGE, ARCHITECTURE AND ARTS

The barbarian invasions into the Western Roman Empire in the 4th and 5th centuries destroyed Roman rule after centuries of full dominance. However, what we do not always realize, but becomes clear when we pay a little more attention to our surroundings, is that the influence of these people is still very much present in our daily lives. A good example is the fact that we continue to use Roman numerals in many situations.

Nevertheless, the legacy of Rome goes far beyond and is present in contemporary Western cultures, especially in the legal and linguistic domains. We cannot forget the Roman heritage in architecture, engineering and even in the field of arts. We are not exempt from it even when we encounter our calendar daily.

These distinctive traits of this civilization were preserved largely due to the establishment of the Germanic kingdoms. These populations absorbed profound Roman cultural aspects in the Middle Ages when they dominated the region of the Western Empire. These characteristics were further retained in Medieval Europe and, starting from the 16th century - the age of great voyages and discoveries -, they began to spread to some regions of Asia, Africa and the Americas.

LATIN

If today we can communicate using, for instance, the Portuguese language both in speech and in writing, we owe it almost exclusively to Latin, the language of Ancient Rome. After the fall of the Western Roman Empire and the invasion of the Germanic tribes into Europe, Portuguese was one of the languages that originated from Latin. The other offspring of the language are French, Italian, Spanish and Romanian.

Latin is nothing more than an Indo-European language. It is believed to have emerged in the 6th century BC in the region of Latium, near the city of Rome. In addition to taking over the entire Roman Empire, it was later adopted by the Roman Catholic Church. During the period known as the Middle Ages, Latin was widely used in most regions. Today, no country in the world speaks the language, but many consider it not entirely dead. The truth, however, is that very few people around the world, mostly scholars of ancient languages and religious individuals, are proficient in Latin.

Portuguese was the last language formed from Latin. The poem "Portuguese Language", by Olavo Bilac, makes this reference quite clear: "Last flower of the Latium, wild and sweet/ Thou art, at once, both sepulture and splendour: Hidden in slag, a gold of native grandeur/ Which crude mines veil among the muddy grit...". (translated by Pedro Mohallem)

The Roman alphabet is still used today in most countries around the globe. Even languages that are not of Latin origin, like German, for example, make use of it.

Roman numerals have also reached us, established and used in Ancient Rome. We use them today in various situations. The Roman numeral system in the Latin alphabet consists of seven uppercase letters: I, V, X, L, C, D, and M.

ROMAN CALENDAR

Calendars were devised in many societies due to the need for measuring time. Over the years, this mechanism assumed the role of a primary guide of life in various aspects. People from different cultures assigned functions to specific days and years. That is, calendars also gained a strong cultural character and were linked to aspects such as beliefs and religiosity.

The most primitive calendars were the Hebrew and the Egyptian. Both had a year consisting of precisely 360 days. According to some historians, around 5,000 BCE, after several reforms, the Egyptians established a civil year of 365 days without variation. The approximate delay of six hours per year compared to the tropical year, which lasts about 365.24219 days, caused the Egyptian seasons to slowly fall behind. The introduction of the first Roman calendar is attributed to the legendary founder of the city, Romulus. In fact, its construction is closely intertwined with the origin of Rome (753 BCE).

The calendar only took the format we know today in the period of emperor Caesar Augustus

Interestingly, the early Roman calendar had only 10 months and 304 days. In this calendar, the first four months were named after Roman mythological gods (Martius, Aprilis, Maius and Junius), while the remaining months were designated by ordinal numbers: Quintilis, Sextilis, September, October, November and December. It is important to note that this calendar had no astronomical basis since the periods had no relation to the solar or lunar movements.

NUMA POMPILIUS

Only the second Roman king, Numa Pompilius (715-673 BCE), established a calendar based on the movements of the Sun and the Moon. As a result, the year had 355 days properly distributed across 12 months. Since he considered months with an even number of days "unlucky", he decided to remove one day from each month that had 30 days. He then took these six extra days and combined them with an additional 50 days to create two new months: Januarius and Februarius. The latter, with 28 days, was dedicated to Februa, a deity who purified the dead. Romans offered sacrifices to her to atone for their sins throughout the year. Because of this, Februarius was established as the last month.

JULIAN CALENDAR

However, the Romans began to recognize the importance of coordinating their lunar year with the changing seasons. To achieve this, they established an early solar-lunar system, in which they added a new month called Mercedonius to their calendar every two years. This new month lasted for 22 or 23 days. It resulted in years of 377 and 378 days between years with only 355 days. When averaged every four years, this came out to 366.25 days, one extra day in relation to the so-called tropical year.

These intercalations with the month Mercedonius, however, began to occur according to political interests. In general, the pontiffs often increased or shortened the year based on their affection toward those in power at the time. This situation led to so much confusion that at one point, the beginning of the year was nearly three months ahead of the climatic seasons.

Upon coming to power in Rome, Julius Caesar decided to eliminate the problem once and for all. The new emperor appointed the Greek astronomer Sosigenes to assess the chaotic situation. The expert concluded that the Roman calendar was 67 days ahead when compared to the seasons.

As a result, Julius Caesar ordered that in 46 BCE, in addition to Mercedonius, two more months would be instituted: one with 33 days and another with 34 days, totaling a civil year of 445 days, the longest ever recorded. This became widely known as the Year of Confusion.

From 45 BCE onwards, the Julian calendar – also known as solar calendar -was adopted. It was developed through a system that unfolded in cycles of four years, with three common years of 365 days and a leap year of 366 days. The leap year aimed to compensate for the nearly six--hour difference from the tropical year. Mercedonius was eliminated, and Februarius was relocated to the second month of the year. In tribute to Julius Caesar, the month Quintilis was renamed Julius.

CALENDAR OF AUGUSTUS

The Roman calendar would only reach the format still used today in the year 730 of Rome. At that time, the Senate, through a decree, decided to rename Sextilis to Augustus, as it was during that month that the then-emperor Caesar Augustus put an end to the civil war that had been afflicting the Roman population. To ensure that the month of Augustus had no fewer days than Julius (dedicated to Julius Caesar), the eighth month of the year was extended to 31 days. The additional day was taken from Februarius, which would have 28 days in common years and 29 in leap years.

This change led to other adjustments. To avoid having several months in a row with 31 days, September and November were reduced to 30 days. Consequently, October and December gained an extra day and they now have 31 days. Even though it may not seem very logical, this distribution of days and months continues to be used today. The names of the months were simply translated into their respective languages.

POLITICS

While the imperial period certainly marked Rome as a massive power, a significant portion of its history was written under the republican sys-

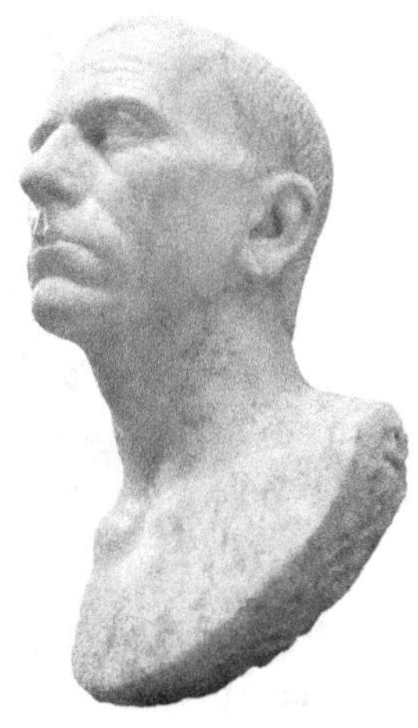

Bust of Roman senator: legislative power in Ancient Rome was composed of 300 patricians

tem. From the 6th century BCE until 27 BCE, the republic was the political system used as administration. The Latin expression "res publica" translates to "public thing" or "public affair". Thus, in theory, it was a form of government linked to the people, but not to the entire Roman population. During this era, those who held power were the patricians.

The Roman Senate, in fact, was composed of 300 patricians and one of its functions was to elect a consul to govern the Republic for a specified period. Below the senators were the magistracies through which magistrates performed various public functions. There were also assemblies or comitia, with three types: Curiata, Tributa and Centuriata. The Comitia Centuriata was the most important as it included the soldiers, making it a political power of the military.

The different divisions and functions were perhaps the most significant Roman legacies to contemporary politics. Such a vast territorial expanse could not be managed by just a few, and the various strategies developed over the centuries - including the imperial period - were of fundamental importance for maintaining governance.

Moreover, during the Republic, there was a class struggle between the less privileged and the holders of power. The system of that period allowed for greater representation of the less privileged in politics. Despite flaws in the execution of the republican system, it was when the people had a bit more active voice in politics.

ECONOMY

Some of the cornerstones of the Roman economy during the imperial period were craftsmanship and mining. The conquests of neighboring lands allowed Rome to make a significant shift from an agrarian economy to a mercantile one, with trade becoming the dominant system in the economic sphere.

This model was widely spread around the world, and today, many countries rely on trade as a substantial source of income. Additionally, Rome instituted mandatory taxation as a means to support the public machinery.

LAW

The rulers of Rome needed to create mechanisms to keep order within the vast Empire over the centuries. To achieve this, they developed laws, which later gave rise to legal codes. Thus, Roman law, which was used as a foundation by future Western societies, was born. Obviously, these norms and regulations underwent various adaptations and changes over the years.

Roman law was essentially divided into three distinct categories: public law (laws directed at citizens), private law (laws for families) and foreign law. The civil code, quite common in Western nations today, originated from public law.

Furthermore, many legal expressions used in the legislations of various countries today were coined in Roman law and, for this reason, are written in Latin, the official language of the Empire. Some examples include habeas corpus, habeas data (an action that ensures citizens' access to information about themselves), stricto sensu (strict sense), juris tantum (presumption of innocence), vacatio legis (legal period in which a law has to come into effect), among many others.

Roman law began in the period of the city's foundation (753 BCE) and extended until the death of the last emperor, Justinian, in 565 CE. In these centuries, the body of Roman law established itself as one of the most important legal systems ever created.

STAGES OF THE ROMAN LAW

The development of Roman law throughout history occurred in distinct stages, leading to a continuous refinement of the legal process. The first period of the Roman law was the Regal period, which began with the founding of Rome and continued until the 5th century BCE, during the republican system. In this period, the law was primarily based on custom, with sacred law closely linked to human law.

The following period was the Republican period, spanning from 510 BCE to the beginning of the imperial era in 27 BCE when Augustus ruled the great power. In this stage, the jus gentium (peoples' right) prevailed over jus fas (sacred right). It was a legal system common to all the peoples of the Mediterranean. Concepts of "law and justice" and good faith were also prevalent during this time.

The Principate period was the era of classical law, a golden age of jurisprudence, which lasted from the reign of Augustus until the end of the 3rd century under Emperor Diocletian. At this time, legal experts known as jurisconsults played a much more significant role in the development of law.

Finally, Roman law experienced the period of Absolute Monarchy in the 4th century CE, following the rule of Emperor Diocletian. This regime continued until the death of Emperor Justinian in the 6th century. It marked the era of the post-classical law, characterized by the absence of prominent jurisconsults and the adaptation of laws to the new official religion, Christianity. In this period, the formation of modern law began and it started to be codified from the 6th century by Justinian.

ENGINEERING AND ARCHITECTURE

One of the main contributions made by Rome was the development of various architectural and engineering techniques for constructing grand buildings, palaces, basilicas, stadiums, amphitheaters, as well as public buildings. The Romans demonstrated such efficiency that many of the constructions from that era have endured to the present day.

Aqueducts, for example, added to the beauty of the Roman landscape. These structures - resembling large stone bridges with arches and columns - were responsible for transporting water to the cities. They were so sturdy that some are still in use today, such as the aqueducts in Spain, built during Emperor Augustus' time.

It can also be said that Roman cities had a perfect urban plan, structured around straight streets intersecting at right angles. This Roman urban model was imposed throughout the regions encompassed by the Empire, with forums, triumphal arches, baths and temples.

Roads were another specialty of the Romans. They connected the capital to the numerous provinces under their control. They enabled the rapid transportation of goods and were crucial to the economic development of the Empire.

The techniques for developing these structures were widely adopted by subsequent societies. Even the study of physics (applied to engineering) advanced. As a result, Roman influence is still evident in buildings, houses and churches to this day.

ARTS

The Romans were heavily influenced by the Greeks also in the field of arts. Among the most profound characteristics from Greece that made their way to Rome were the realistic depiction of the human body and elements of nature.

Although realism in sculptures and paintings was sidelined in the Middle Ages, it was later revived during the Renaissance and preserved by different art movements and schools.

The earliest Roman sculptures were actually developed by Greeks and Eastern people living in Rome. The exquisite statues of Caesar Augustus and his associates have endured to the present day. The art of the cameo - which involved highlighting a specific figure in a semiprecious stone using the stone's veins and layers of color - reached its peak during the 1st century of the Roman Empire.

Pictorial reliefs received new elements, gaining depth with the introduction of landscapes. On the other hand, in historical reliefs, artists car-

ved scenes of important moments. Notable examples include the well-
-known columns of the emperors Trajan and Hadrian.

During the Republic, portraiture was the most cultivated genre. It was presented in the form of busts and equestrian statues. During the time of Emperor Caesar Augustus, images were produced only until the neck. However, in the 1st century CE, pieces were made up to the middle of the chest. Over time, portraiture became known for its sober realism.

While statues played a significant role, Roman painting did not leave a profound legacy, remaining as a decorative function in architecture. It is important to note that there are not many remnants of this type of art that have reached the Western world. Nevertheless, painting was per-formed on three main surfaces: the book, the wall and the panel. Large walls mainly emerged through the decoration of churches. Mosaics, on the other hand, had a significant presence in Rome, both in wall decora-tion and floor paving.

ENRICHING

The Greeks are much more famous for their intellectual and creati-ve genius in Antiquity. However, even though they did not achieve such a level of creative capacity, the Romans managed to assimilate, enrich and spread the Hellenic heritage throughout the West. Thus, the Greco-Roman cultural tradition was never completely lost, as it can be seen during the Renaissance period. Rome's legacy is present in countless disciplines, and the organizational model of the Empire remains a true lesson for us even nowadays. Therefore, there is no doubt that our society would not have reached the level of cultural growth and maturity without the aid of this important society, which established its dominance in the ancient world.

www.ingramcontent.com/pod-product-compliance
Lightning Source LLC
LaVergne TN
LVHW060352200726

843506LV00003B/197